Shakespeare Alive

William Shakespeare: A Man for All Times

D1486652

Paul Shuter

Raintree is an imprint of Capstone Global Library Limited, a company incorporated in England and Wales having its registered office at 7 Pilgrim Street, London, EC4V 6LB – Registered company number: 6695582

www.raintreepublishers.co.uk
myorders@raintreepublishers.co.uk

Text © Capstone Global Library Limited 2014
First published in hardback in 2014
The moral rights of the proprietor have been asserted.

Edited by Andrew Farrow and Abby Colich
Designed by Steve Mead
Original illustrations © Capstone Global
   Library Ltd 2014
Picture research by Elizabeth Alexander
Production by Victoria Fitzgerald
Originated by Capstone Global Library Ltd
Printed and bound in China

ISBN 978 1 406 27331 1
17 16 15 14 13
10 9 8 7 6 5 4 3 2 1

British Library Cataloguing in Publication Data
Shuter, Paul
William Shakespeare: A Man for all Times. – (Shakespeare Alive)
A full catalogue record for this book is available from the British Library.

Chatsworth Reproduced by permission of Chatsworth Settlement Trustees), 37 (British Library, London, UK / © British Library Board. All Rights Reserved); © The British Library Board: pp. 32 (C.21.c.45), 46 (Add.70438 f.18), 65 (Maps.M.T.61.(12)); Capstone Global Library: pp. 6 (Trevor Clifford), 16 (Trevor Clifford), 17 (Trevor Clifford); Carlos Lemos@MOLA: p. 25; Corbis: pp. 29 (© Robbie Jack), 43 (© Jason Hawkes); Getty Images: p. 19 (Archive Photos); McCurdy & Co: p. 40; The National Archives, ref AO3/908/13 (2v): p. 53; The National Archives, ref PROB 1/4: pp. 66, 67; Paul & Jane Shuter Ltd.: pp. 10, 27, 45, 68; By Permission of the Shakespeare Birthplace Trust: p. 9; Shakespeare's Globe: p. 35 (photograph by John Tramper, 2012), 38 (photograph by John Haynes, 2010), 58 (photograph by John Haynes, 2008), 61 (photograph by Marc Brenner, 2013), 70 (photograph by Ellie Kurttz, 2012); Shutterstock: p. 15 (© James Kingman); Superstock: p. 12 (Bridgeman Art Library, London); TopFoto.co.uk: pp. 55 (City of London / HIP), 63 (The Granger Collection); Utrecht, University Library, formerly Ms. 1198 f. 83, now Gr. form. 12: p. 21.

Design features: Shutterstock (© R-studio), (© David M. Schrader), (© Tribalium), (© tkada), (© Valentin Agapov).

Cover photograph of the Droeshout frontpiece to the first complete quarto edition of the works of William Shakespeare,1623, reproduced with permission from Getty Images (Rischgitz/Hulton Archive).

We would like to thank Farah Karim-Cooper for her invaluable help in the preparation of this book.

The author would like to thank Patrick Spotiswoode and Hilary Crain for their comments on the first draft of this manuscript. Philip Hall, agricultural valuer at Savills Banbury office, helped me understand the value of the land Shakespeare bought.Every effort has been made to contact copyright holders of material reproduced in this book. Any omissions will be rectified in subsequent printings if notice is given to the publisher.

Contents

Some words are shown in bold, **like this**. You can find out what they mean by looking in the glossary.

Who was Shakespeare?

In 1999, listeners to a BBC radio news programme voted William Shakespeare the "British Person of the Millennium". When the Chinese leader Wen Jiabao visited Britain in 2011, he made a point of saying he had read Shakespeare's *King Lear*, and said Shakespeare was the greatest writer who ever lived.[1] People all over the modern world recognize the image of his face shown on page 5.

Many people, who have spent years reading about it, insist that Shakespeare was a fraud who didn't write the plays that bear his name. Sigmund Freud believed the Earl of Oxford wrote them. Some great Shakespearean actors, like Mark Rylance and Derek Jacobi, insist there is "reasonable doubt" about the authorship of the plays.

How can this be? This isn't a book about the theories of who wrote the plays. It is a biography – a form of history. History is a subject with strict rules about acceptable evidence and how it can be used. We will follow these rules, and I will try to make you aware of them as we go along.

Myth   The Earl of Oxford wrote Shakespeare's plays

Some people say the facts of Shakespeare's life are not those expected for a great writer. The compassionate author of *The Merchant of Venice* would not sue people for small debts. Such a writer would not retire to Stratford to "devote himself to houses, lands, orchards, money, and malt, leaving no traces of a single intellectual or literary interest". On the other hand, the Earl of Oxford went to university. He travelled a lot in Europe and knew many of the places that appear in the plays. The events of his life fit with the stories and information in the plays. To judge whether this is true or not, you need to know more about Shakespeare, so we will come back to this in the **epilogue** (pages 70–71).

The idea Shakespeare didn't write the plays doesn't just crop up in non-fiction. There are films and novels built around it as well. One interesting example is Elise Boach's novel for young adults, *Shakespeare's Secret*. In it, the heroine learns, "Shakespeare couldn't even spell his own name", so she decides, "Okay, so maybe he didn't write the plays".[2] This is fine in fiction, but it breaks the rules of history. In fact, six of Shakespeare's signatures survive, and he does spell his name in different ways. This doesn't mean Shakespeare was dyslexic or stupid. When he was alive, the idea of standard spelling didn't exist. He might spell his name in different ways in just the same way people might pronounce names with different stresses in different circumstances today. It is an example of an anachronism – using an idea from one period of time and applying it to another. This is always wrong in history.

This book will highlight myths, facts, and important points about the world in which Shakespeare lived. My view of who wrote the plays is given away in the evidence and myths boxes in this chapter. Reading the book will give you the evidence to agree with me – or not.

SHAKESPEARE'S WORLD EXPLAINED

Money then and now
In Shakespeare's England, there were 12 pennies in a shilling, and 20 shillings in one pound. It is hard to compare the value of money then and now. There is a table on page 73, which compares a number of prices. For a very rough rule of thumb, multiply prices by 1,000 and wages by 5,000.

Where did Shakespeare come from?

What sort of family did William Shakespeare grow up in? The first family member we know of is Richard Shakespeare, William's grandfather. By 1529, he lived in Snitterfield, a village outside Stratford-upon-Avon. Richard was a **tenant** farmer. He rented his land from Robert Arden, from the nearby village of Wilmcote. Richard was a step down the social scale from men who farmed their own land. He was successful and well thought of by his neighbours, often chosen to value a person's goods after they died. When Richard himself died in 1561, his goods were valued at £38.17s. This was £5 more than the goods of the vicar, one of the most important people in Snitterfield.

This is John Shakespeare's house in Henley Street today. The left half was the first part he owned. He bought the half on the right with two **gables** in 1556.

Richard had at least two sons, Henry and John. Henry became a farmer, but John had other plans. He went to Stratford, as **apprentice** to a glover and **whittawer**. To learn a skilled trade, boys were contracted to a craftsman for seven years, living in the master's house or workshop, and receiving almost no pay.

By 1552, John was living and running his own business as a glover in Henley Street, Stratford. We know because he was fined for having his own dung heap rather than using the official one at the end of the street! His house in Henley Street was half of the house now called Shakespeare's Birthplace.[1]

John was successful. In 1556, he bought the other half of the Henley Street house and another house in Stratford, which he rented out. A successful man with his own house and business needs a wife, and between 1556 and 1558 he found one – Mary Arden.

The Arden family

Mary was the daughter of Robert Arden, Richard Shakespeare's landlord. The Ardens were higher up the social scale than the Shakepeares – Robert owned a number of farms. He died in 1556 or early 1557. Mary was the youngest of eight daughters and wasn't married when Robert died. He trusted her despite her being a daughter and his youngest, and made her one of the two **executors** of his will. He left her his most valuable farm and money. Sometime after Robert's death, and before the birth of their first child in September 1558, Mary and the up-and-coming John Shakespeare were married.

Myth
Mary Arden lived at Mary Arden's Farm

The Shakespeare's Birthplace Trust owns a series of properties associated with Shakespeare and his family in and around Stratford. Mary Arden's Farm in Wilmcote is one of them. However, there is no proof this is where she grew up. A local historian, John Jordan, first claimed that this house was the Arden's home over 200 years later. He gave no evidence for his claim. Jordan made part of his living by guiding early tourists around the Shakespeare sites, and arranging for them to buy "authentic" souvenirs. It was in his interests to have another site to visit.[2]

Whether it is the actual house Mary grew up in or not doesn't matter very much. It was the house of a well-off family, and if the Ardens didn't live in this one, they probably lived in one like it. There is a video showing the Shakespeare properties on the Shakespeare Birthplace Trust website (see page 78).

John Shakespeare's success

John soon became an important man in Stratford. The town was run by a bailiff (like a mayor), senior councillors called aldermen, and junior councillors called burgesses. From 1556, he had three junior jobs in the Stratford administration. In about 1560, he made it on to the Council, elected as a burgess. From 1561 to 1566, he was one of the two men responsible for the town's finances. In 1565, he became an alderman, and in 1568, he was elected bailiff, running the town. He was trusted and well respected. In 1572, John Shakespeare and a neighbour, Adrian Quiney, went to London on the town's business. They were given the power to make whatever decisions seemed best to them.

Historians often say John Shakespeare could not read or write. He used a mark rather than signing his name. However, Adrian Quiney usually made a mark, too, and we have letters Quiney wrote himself. So Quiney could read and write, but at the same time signed his name with a mark. John could have done the same, so the evidence is not conclusive.

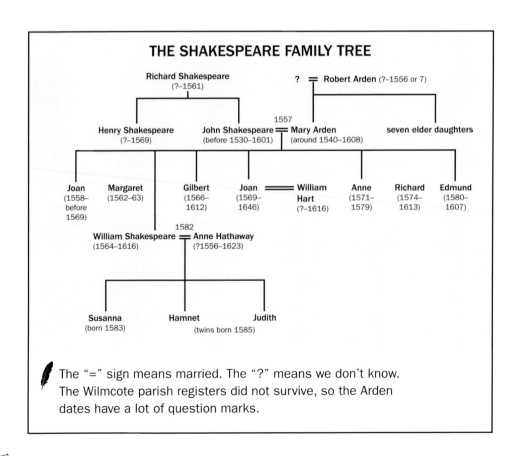

THE SHAKESPEARE FAMILY TREE

Richard Shakespeare (?–1561)

? = **Robert Arden** (?–1556 or 7)

1557

Henry Shakespeare (?–1569)

John Shakespeare (before 1530–1601) = **Mary Arden** (around 1540–1608)

seven elder daughters

Joan (1558– before 1569)

Margaret (1562–63)

Gilbert (1566– 1612)

Joan (1569– 1646) = **William Hart** (?–1616)

Anne (1571– 1579)

Richard (1574– 1613)

Edmund (1580– 1607)

1582

William Shakespeare (1564–1616) = **Anne Hathaway** (?1556–1623)

Susanna (born 1583)

Hamnet **Judith** (twins born 1585)

The "=" sign means married. The "?" means we don't know. The Wilmcote parish registers did not survive, so the Arden dates have a lot of question marks.

John and Mary's children

The Shakespeares had eight children, of which William was the third. It is possible both his elder **siblings** were dead by 1564, when William was born. Joan, the eldest, died before 1569, when another daughter was given the same name. Many parents did this at the time.

William must have been a tough child. When he was young, about 16 per cent of children died in the first year of their lives. The first year of William's life was worse than most. Plague broke out in Stratford on 11 July 1564, and over 200 died in a town of not much more than 1,000 people. One family who lived near the Shakespeares lost four children.[3]

WHAT'S THE EVIDENCE?

Baptism

A new law in 1538 meant each **parish** had to keep records, called registers, of all the local baptisms, marriages, and funerals. Some parishes, such as Stratford, kept quite good records, which have survived. The fourth line in the register under the year 1564 says:

April 26 Gulielmus filius Johannes Shakespere

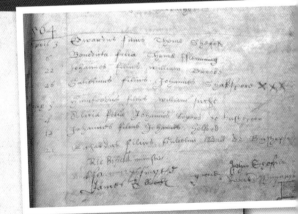

Later, somebody added the XXX to show people where to look.[4] Clergymen wrote the registers in Latin. Translated, it says:

William son of John Shakespere

During Shakespeare's life, people didn't worry much about spelling – his name is spelt many different ways.

Elizabethan grammar schools

There are still schools called grammar schools in Britain and the United States today. But they are nothing like the Elizabethan grammar schools. These schools really were what they said they were: schools that taught grammar – and Latin grammar, at that. Latin was the language of education, of learning, often of the law, and of international trade – it was everybody's second language throughout Europe. Men like John Shakespeare may or may not have been able to read and write, but they wanted education to give their sons a chance to rise in the world. That meant understanding Latin.

In Stratford, boys learned to read and write before they went to grammar school (at about seven years old). School days were long: from six in the morning (seven in winter) to eleven, then home for lunch, back at one, and the day ended at five. Also, there were no terms. The year was broken up by holidays lasting one or two days, but school was twelve months a year.[5]

The school would usually be in one room, with the master teaching the older boys, and an assistant teaching the younger ones. Discipline was harsh. Flogging with the **birch** was quite normal.

Lessons

Rote learning was important. At the age of seven, boys had to learn three Latin words a day; by ten, they would be learning whole Latin books. Some of the things they learned was ideal training for a boy who would be a playwright:

- **Rhetoric** – speaking and writing effectively.
- **Synonyms** – finding different ways of saying the same thing, for example, 150 ways to say thank you for your letter – in Latin of course.[6]
- Impersonations – writing in the character of another person, for example writing as Queen Dido in the classical story where she falls in love with and then loses Aeneas, a hero from Troy.
- Performance – in many schools, the boys did not just study Roman plays in Latin, they acted them, to help the students understand them.

So Shakespeare's education taught him a lot about writing, about the stories and myths of Rome, about **empathy**, and may even have started him acting.

WHAT'S THE EVIDENCE?

Did Shakespeare go to school?
There are no documents that prove William Shakespeare went to school. The evidence we have is:

- ◆ In his later life, Shakespeare was an educated man.
- ◆ There was a school in Stratford that the sons of men like John Shakespeare went to.
- ◆ No lists of pupils from the Stratford school survive.

So historians **infer** Shakespeare went to the school. The rule for historians is to use as few inferences as possible. So in this case, the simplest inference is that a boy of his social status went to his local school. A more complicated scenario would be that he impressed a visiting nobleman who took him away to be privately educated in his house. Shakespeare going to school in Stratford only needs one inference. The second example needs three inferences – he met a nobleman, the nobleman was impressed, and the nobleman took him away to be educated. One inference is always better in history than three.

FACT

26 April 1564 William Shakespeare baptized. His father, John Shakespeare, was a successful local businessman.

After school... marriage

We don't know when Shakespeare left school. The usual age to leave was about 15. We also don't know what he did next. We do know he didn't go on to university. It would be normal for a youth from a family like the Shakespeares to start working with his father, and that may be what he did.

His father probably needed the help. John's business was not going very well. He was not only a glover, but also a wool **speculator** and a money lender. Things went wrong around 1576 (when William was 12). The first sign was, having only missed one Council meeting in the previous 13 years, he stopped going. His colleagues on the Council gave him plenty of time to recover, only replacing him as an alderman in 1586. In 1592, John was on a list of people who did not go to church at least once a month. This could show he was a Roman Catholic, but the list itself says the reason was probably fear of being arrested for debt.[1]

Queen Elizabeth I reigned from 1558 until her death in 1603. This time is known as the Elizabethan era.

A Catholic family?

There is another reason for thinking John Shakespeare might have been a Roman Catholic. In 1757, when workers were repairing the roof of his house in Henley Street, they found a small booklet. This booklet is a Roman Catholic confession of faith, a list of 14 beliefs that Roman Catholics accepted, and Protestants didn't. For example: "Item, I John Shakspear doe protest that I will also passe out of this life, armed with the last sacrament of extreme unction."[2]

The booklet no longer survives. It may have been a forgery, but it could have been genuine. The text is very close to the *Testament of Faith* that secret Roman Catholic priests who visited England in the 1580s gave to their supporters. In 1581, one of them wrote to headquarters in Rome: "Father Robert wants three or four thousand or more of the Testaments, for many people desire to have them."[3] So a secret Roman Catholic might have a version of the Testament. Father Robert's would have been printed, not handwritten. If John Shakespeare could not read or write, then he couldn't have copied it. We can't be sure. And, of course, even if John Shakespeare was a secret Roman Catholic, it doesn't mean William was.

SHAKESPEARE'S WORLD EXPLAINED

Religion and politics

Shakespeare's father, John, was born when the country was Roman Catholic. However, he lived through the **Reformation**.

- Henry VIII (1509–1547) broke with Rome and the Pope in 1533. England became Protestant, although a lot of old ideas were kept.
- Edward VI (ruled 1547–1553) made the country more strongly Protestant.
- Mary I (1553–1559) took the country back to Roman Catholicism. During her reign, Protestants were persecuted, and some were burnt for **heresy**.
- Elizabeth I (1559–1603) took the country back to moderate Protestantism. Her government did not persecute Roman Catholics if they "conformed". This meant going to Protestant church services at least once a month.

There was a political side to this. Governments decided the people's religion, but many people's religious faith was more important than their loyalty to the monarch. Elizabeth avoided persecuting Catholics at first. After the Pope excommunicated her in 1570, telling English Catholics they should rebel against her, Catholic priests were tracked down and prosecuted for **treason**. The Spanish Armada (1588) was an attempt to invade England and make it Roman Catholic again.

Marriage

Men usually married when they were in their late twenties, and women were usually two or three years younger than their husbands. Arranged marriages were common among people like the Shakespeares. Parents, especially the woman's parents, often played an important part in setting them up. Once she was married, all that a woman owned became her husband's. Women usually brought a **dowry** (money or property) to the marriage, and their father negotiated a marriage contract. This set out what she would bring, but also how she would be supported if her husband died first.

Before the couple could marry, they had to have the **banns** called. For three successive Sundays or **holy days**, during the service, the minister announced their plan to marry. If there was a reason why they should not marry (such as one of them was already married), this gave people time to object. There were times during the year when banns could not be called, and in 1582, this included from 2 December through to 13 January 1583.[4] If people wanted to marry without normal banns, they needed a licence from the local bishop.

Shakespeare gets married

William Shakespeare wanted to get married in November 1582, and he left it too late to have the normal banns read. He was 18, very young for marriage at the time. To get a special licence, you needed a sworn document giving the names, addresses, and consent of all the relevant people. In William's case, this included his father because he was not yet 21, the age when he could decide for himself. You also needed another document declaring there was no reason why the couple should not marry, and a **bond** promising to pay a fine if a problem was discovered later. If all the paperwork was correct, the bishop's court would issue a licence allowing a minister to marry the couple, and make a note in the register. This note appears in the Bishop of Worcester's register: "27 November 1582: [a marriage licence] between William Shaxpere and Anne Whateley of Temple Grafton."[5] Temple Grafton is a village about 8 kilometres (5 miles) west of Stratford. None of the paperwork survives except bond: "28 November ... that William Shagspere on th one partie, and Anne Hathwey of Stratford in the diocese of Worcester, maiden, may lawfully solemnize matrimony together."[6]

This is the house where Anne Hathaway grew up. Known today as Anne Hathaway's Cottage, it was known then as Hewlands Farm. As we can still see, it was the large house of a prosperous family.

Which Anne?

There is a lot of evidence which shows Shakespeare married Anne Hathaway, and no evidence apart from the register entry that Anne Whatley even existed. William and Anne's fathers knew one another. Anne's father died in 1581, and she would inherit money when she married. Her mother was already dead, so she was more independent than most women at the time. Her brother had taken over the family home, but Anne and her stepmother still lived there. She was older than William, probably 27, and she was three months pregnant.

The pregnancy explains the need to get married quickly, although it wasn't that unusual. Perhaps as many as one in three brides at the time were pregnant.[7] How do we explain Anne Whatley though? The most likely answer is that it was a mistake by the clerk who wrote up the register. He took notes during the session, and wrote them up afterwards. Earlier the same day, there had been a case involving William Whatley before the court. Temple Grafton may have been the church where the couple were to marry.

Children

Soon the Stratford parish registers record: "[1583] May 26 Susanna daughter to William Shakspere". While Shakespeare's father may have had Roman Catholic beliefs, Anne Hathaway's family seem to have had **Puritan** ones. Susanna was a popular name amongst Puritan families, because of the story of Susanna in the Bible.[8]

Twenty months later, the parish registers have more news: "[1585] February 2 Hamnet and Judith sonne and daughter to William Shakspere". The twins were named after family friends, Hamnet and Judith Sadler, who were bakers in Stratford's High Street. Later, the Sadlers returned the compliment, naming their son William. As we have seen, Elizabethans didn't worry much about spelling, and "Hamnet "and "Hamlet" were two ways of writing the same name. Hamnet Sadler is also called "Hambnet" and "Hamlet" in the Stratford records.

Shakespeare's Birthplace is furnished with modern copies of old furniture and painted cloths. Here you can see the table, a bench, a stool, and a settle – a bench like a wooden sofa.

This jointed bed, with curtains for privacy, can also be seen at Shakespeare's Birthplace. Pulled out from underneath it is a truckle bed, for one or more of the children. The mattress rested on a network of ropes. When they started to sag, the bed was uncomfortable and the ropes could be tightened up. Our phrase "sleep tight" comes from this.

Home life

As William was so young, he and Anne probably lived with his parents at their house in Henley Street. Remember, this was John Shakespeare's workplace, as well as the family home. There was much less privacy than we expect today.

To us, an Elizabethan home would seem to have very little furniture. What there was would be handmade. It lasted a long time and was passed down through the generations. A family like the Shakespeares would have a table with enough benches, stools, and chairs for the family to sit round it. The seats were made of oak. People decorated the main rooms with hangings called painted cloths. These were made from linen painted with bright patterns.

FACTS

c. **29 November 1582** William Shakespeare and Anne Hathaway get a licence to marry.
26 May 1583 Susanna Shakespeare baptized.
2 February 1585 Hamnet and Judith Shakespeare baptized.

What happened next?

We are now at what Shakespeare biographers call "the lost years". In 1585, when Shakespeare was 21, the twins were baptized in Stratford. The next time we know anything about him, he was a playwright in London in 1592. So where was he for the missing seven years? We don't even know it was seven years. He and Anne could have gone away after the birth of Susanna, and she (or they) could have just come back to Stratford for the twins to be born.

At some point, he became involved in the theatre. Shakespeare was probably an actor before he became a playwright. Even his early plays show he had a great understanding of what worked on stage.

Myth

Shakespeare left Stratford because he was caught poaching Sir Robert Lucy's deer at Charlecote.

This story was being told in Stratford late in the 17th century, so over 70 years after Shakespeare died in 1616.[1] Some people who knew Shakespeare might still have been alive, but a 15-year-old when Shakespeare died would be in his or her eighties or nineties by then. Nobody was alive from the time when Shakespeare left Stratford in the 1580s so, first of all, the story doesn't have a good source. Second, Sir Robert Lucy didn't have a deer park in Charlecote in the 1580s, but there was one there a hundred years later in the 1680s when the story was first recorded.

Later visitors to Stratford who asked about Shakespeare were often told that he was a big drinker and had once been so drunk after an evening in one of the villages outside Stratford that he couldn't walk home and slept under a tree. For a fee, a guide would show them the tree or sell them a souvenir cut from it. These types of legends often grow up around great men and women. They suggest that local people know the "real" person. In this case, people may have come from London wanting to know about Shakespeare the great writer, but people in Stratford said they knew the *real* Shakespeare. The one they know was a "good lad" – drinking, poaching, and getting into trouble like other young men.

Parts of the Shakespeare myth, like the poaching story, have often been believed. Biographers have made them part of the story. This illustration shows Shakespeare (second from left, standing) caught with the deer. Strangely, Shakespeare seems to be wearing his best clothes.

When did Shakespeare first see professional plays?

In the 1560s, there were no permanent theatres. Professional actors belonged to companies with noble **patrons**. They performed at their patron's house, and (the best ones) at the Queen's **court**. They also toured around the country. These travelling players often visited Stratford. We know this because the town accounts have records of money paid to them. When travelling players arrived in a town, they made a big entrance. They formed a procession in their grand clothes, led by drums and trumpets, and marched to the mayor's house. They showed the mayor their licence from their patron, and asked permission to perform in the town. In 1569, when Shakespeare was five, his father was the bailiff (mayor), so the procession would have come to his home. A boy also born in 1564 described an event like this in nearby Gloucester:

> *My father took me with him, and made me stand between his legs, as he sat on one of the benches, where we saw and heard very well. This sight took such an impression on me that [years later] it was as fresh in my memory as if I had seen it newly acted.*[2]

Filling the lost years

In 1592, Shakespeare was a man of the theatre in London. In 1583 and 1585, he was a young husband and father in Stratford. Biographers have a problem. They look for explanations of how this change happened. Those who believe the poaching myth often believe another myth, that Shakespeare's first job in the theatre was as a horse-holder. This was the equivalent of a modern valet-parking attendant. Others, seeing how much he knows about the law or soldiering in the plays, suggest he must have been a lawyer's clerk or a soldier. The best answer will not need too many inferences (see page 11), and will help explain his success in the theatre. Let's look at the two most popular theories.

WHAT'S THE EVIDENCE?

Was Shakespeare in Lancashire?

Shakespeare's last master at Stratford school was a Lancashire man with Catholic connections. Perhaps he knew Shakespeare's father was a secret Catholic, and he got Shakespeare a job as a private tutor or even an actor with a Lancashire Catholic family.

- In 1581, Alexander Hoghton, a Lancashire Catholic gentleman, made a will which mentioned two actors and musicians in his service: one was "William Shakeshafte".
- Hoghton had connections with Lord Strange, whose estates were in Lancashire, and who had a company of players which were one of the main companies in London.
- Strange's Men may have played some of Shakespeare's early plays.

This theory is not impossible. However, the only real evidence, the mention of Shakeshafte, is weak.

- William Shakespeare's name is spelled in lots of different ways, but this would be the only time it was spelled Shakeshafte.
- On the other hand, Shakeshafte was a common Lancashire surname, and there were several families with that name in Preston, the nearest town to Hoghton's estate.
- Shakespeare was only 17 in 1581, which makes him very young to be an important actor, picked out in Hoghton's will. We also know he was back in Stratford in 1582, marrying Anne Hathaway.

Did he join a group of travelling players?

We know travelling players visited Stratford. At some point, he got to know some of them. He joined a company, probably as an actor, and, when the company went to London, so did Shakespeare. There is no hard evidence to prove this theory, but there is evidence that may support, rather than prove, it.

- In 1587, the most famous company, the Queen's Men, toured Oxfordshire and Warwickshire. On 13 June, one of its main actors was killed in a fight with another member of the company in Thame, Oxfordshire. They needed a new actor.
- Shakespeare was connected with members of the Queen's Men later in his career – for example, John Heminges, who was close to Shakespeare for the rest of his working life and is one of the two men responsible for publishing Shakespeare's plays after his death.
- Some of Shakespeare's plays are rewrites of plays the Queen's Men performed in the 1580s (*King John, King Lear, Richard III, Henry V*).

London

However he got there, by 1592 Shakespeare was a successful playwright in London. Scholars still hope to find the evidence that solves the puzzle of the lost years. They may never succeed. Shakespeare certainly understood what worked on the stage. Actors and directors today say even his early plays show this. This means it is likely that he was an actor first, and then a playwright.

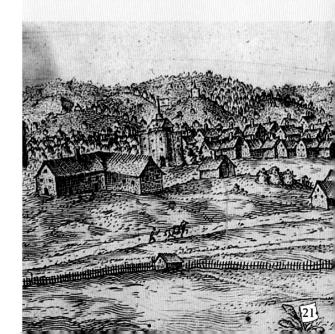

London's first playhouses, the Theatre (built by James Burbage, 1576) and the Curtain (the tall building centre-left, built nearby, c. 1577), were built just outside the City because London's Mayor and Council disapproved.

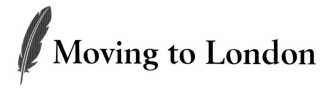

Moving to London

Shakespeare came to London in his early 20s, during the second half of the 1580s. What was the city like?

London

Around 1600, London was by far the largest city in England. About 200,000 people lived there, which made it more than 10 times larger than the next biggest cities. It was the centre for the law and for training lawyers. Westminster, where laws were made and the royal court was based, was a couple of miles west down the River Thames (to the left in the picture). London was the heart of the economy. It was the biggest and busiest port, with the largest ships able to dock anywhere east (right) of the bridge; it was also the most important manufacturing centre in the country.

London grew, both in population and in area, throughout Shakespeare's lifetime. Before the Reformation, there were many monasteries and other religious buildings inside the City, as well as St Paul's Cathedral, and over 100 parish churches. After the Reformation, the new Church of England only used the churches and the Cathedral. King Henry VIII took the monasteries and other church lands and sold or gave them away. Tudor London had its property developers just like modern London, and they flourished in the old Church lands. Much of this land was just outside the old city walls, in the areas called the suburbs, so most of it was outside the control of the Mayor and Council. Called "liberties", they are where the first theatres were built.

What did London look like?

A Dutch artist painted the picture below, probably in the 1620s. He may never have seen London; he was copying an engraving published in 1616 by another Dutchman, Claes Visscher. Visscher probably never saw London either. He based his engraving on one by John Norden, drawn around 1600. So this painting is a copy of a copy. There are mistakes, but it does give us a good idea of the city about 10 years after Shakespeare arrived.

This is London from the south, and it shows how important the river was to the city. To the right, with four domed towers, is the Tower of London. It was a multi-purpose royal site – fortress, prison, royal palace, mint, **armoury**, jewel house, and record repository. Ordinary citizens could get married there and visit the zoo.

The bridge was about 244 metres (800 feet) long, with houses built on arches above the roadway. The lower floors of these houses were shops that opened onto the road. There were only three gaps where you could see the river at all.

St Paul's dominates the centre, a great gothic cathedral later destroyed in the Great Fire of London in 1666. It was more than just a church. In the nave, lawyers met their clients, servants looked for employers, fashionable young men walked about to show off their latest clothes, and tailors displayed their cloth and lace. Deliverymen even used it as a short cut. Outside, the churchyard was the centre of the book industry.

The London theatres

When Shakespeare joined the industry, acting companies toured the country, playing in the bigger towns, and in London, usually in inns. The best acting companies also performed for the Queen. London, with its large population, was the best place for them, but the Mayor and Council tried to keep them out.

To get round the City's opposition, and to avoid splitting the profits with the innkeepers, businessmen built special playhouses, in liberties and suburbs. The most important early ones were the Theatre (1576) and the Curtain (1577), both north of the City. Later, the Rose (1587), the Swan (1595), and the Globe (1599) were built south of the river in an area called Bankside. They were normally built by businessmen, because they needed **capital** to pay the costs of renting or buying the land and paying for the building. The businessman then needed a deal with a playing company to perform in his theatre. The takings usually were shared between the businessman and the company.

What were these buildings like? Each one was slightly different, but they had common features. They were **polygonal**. In the centre there was an open-air yard, where some of the audience stood to watch the play. Jutting into the yard was the stage, perhaps 1.5 metres (5 feet) high. Around the yard were roofed **galleries**, usually three storeys, providing seats, and open on the yard side. Behind the stage was the **tiring house**, where the actors changed and stored their costumes and props. The front of the tiring house was the back wall of the stage. There were usually three doors, one on each side, and a larger one in the middle. They were made from a timber frame, with the outside walls filled in with **lath and plaster**. Thomas Platter, a Swiss tourist, described them in his journal:

> They play on a raised stage, so that everyone has a good view. There are different galleries where the seating is better and more comfortable and therefore more expensive. Those who stand below only pay one English penny, but if you wish to sit, you enter by another door, and pay another penny. If you want to sit in the most comfortable (cushioned) seats, where you not only see everything well, but also can be seen, then you pay yet another penny, at another door. During the performance, food and drink are carried round the audience, so that, for what one cares to pay, one may have refreshment.[1]

The archaeology of the Rose theatre

In 1888–1889, archaeologists found the remains of the Rose theatre. In the plan here, those things marked in black were found, and the lighter lines are what archaeologists infer were there. The whole right-hand side of the Rose is unexcavated. You can see the Rose was a 14-sided polygon (it was not possible to make a circular timber-framed building). The yard sloped towards the stage, both for drainage, and to help the people at the back see. The archaeology can't tell us about the back wall of the stage, and in the drawing it has been left as a timber framework, but it would certainly have been a solid wall with doors. The owners sold food and drink to the playgoers from the building called Cholmley's house.[2]

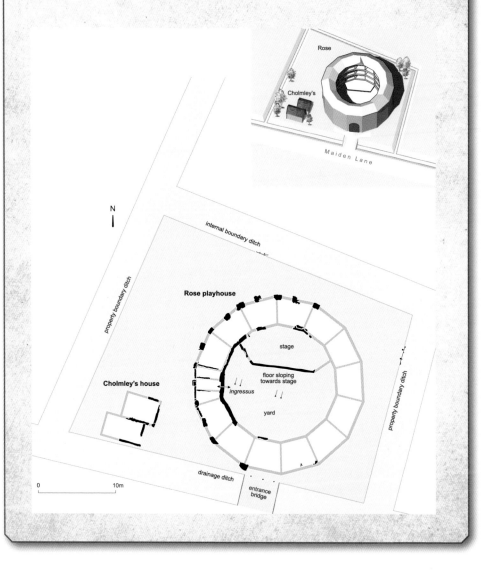

How do we know Shakespeare was an actor and playwright?

The "lost years" end in 1592, when Shakespeare is mentioned in a pamphlet called *Greene's Groats-worth of Witte, bought with a million of repentance. Describing the folly of youth, the falsehood of makeshift flatterers, the misery of the negligent, and mischiefs of deceiving courtesans. Written before his death and published at his dying request.* The title gives you an idea about the whole book. It was sensationalist. There were attacks on both Christopher Marlowe and Shakespeare. This is what it says about Shakespeare:

> there is an upstart Crow, *beautified with our feathers, that with his* Tygers hart wrapt in a Players hide, *supposes he is as well able to bombast out a blanke verse as the best of you: and being an absolute* Johannes fac totum, *is in his owne conceit the onely Shake-scene in a countrie.*[3]

It is far from polite.

- "Upstart" suggests both a very recent success, and that Shakespeare was from a lower social class, or not well educated, unlike Greene and his university-educated friends.

- The crow was thought to only be able to imitate other birds, not make up its own song. Here it means actor, because actors say other people's words ("our feathers").

SHAKESPEARE'S WORLD EXPLAINED

Marlowe's mighty line

The star company of actors in the 1580s were the Queen's Men. Their plays were in verse, which often rhymed. In the late 1580s, new playwrights burst onto the scene, writing a new kind of verse. The most successful was Christopher Marlowe. His new verse, called blank verse, didn't rhyme. The lines were shorter, too – the older plays often used a 14-syllable line, but Marlowe used ten. This is called an iambic pentameter – a line of five pairs of syllables, with the second syllable subtly stressed. The first three lines from Marlowe's first great hit, *Tamburlaine*, show how it worked. Stress the bold parts as you read:

From **jigg**ing **veins** of **rhy**ming **mo**ther-**wits**,
And **such** con**ceits** as **clown**age **keeps** in **pay**,
We'll **lead** you **to** the **state**ly **tent** of **war**.

So no more rhymes, no more clowns, but instead a thrilling story of war and conquest. Shakespeare, who wrote his first plays around the same time, was one of the new men, writing the new blank verse.

- "Tiger's heart wrapped in a Player's hide" was printed in a different typeface in the original, to make clear it was a quote (well, almost) from Shakespeare's *Henry VI Part 3* – where the Duke of York says Queen Margaret has "A tiger's heart wrapped in a woman's hide."
- "*Johannes fac totum*" is Latin. It means the same as the modern "jack-of-all-trades", someone who is good at many things, but not expert in any.
- It ends, "in his own conceit, the only Shake-scene in the country". The pun on Shakespeare's name is obvious, and this suggests he is big-headed, too, and, in his own opinion, the best playwright.

As you can see below, Greene may not have written the *Groats-worth of Witte*, but for our purposes it doesn't matter. It shows that in the late summer of 1592, when he was 28, Shakespeare was already an actor, a playwright, and a success. It is time to look at his first plays.

WHAT'S THE EVIDENCE?

Who wrote the *Groatsworth of Wit*?

Robert Greene was a celebrity writer. He wrote successful plays, romances, and books pretending to expose con men (who he made up). His life was colourful. He had abandoned his pregnant wife and was living with his mistress, a prostitute, in a rough part of town. His death was news, and news sells books. *Groatsworth* and two other books claimed Greene wrote them on his deathbed. Another writer, Henry Chettle, admitted preparing the *Groatsworth* for the press, and computer analysis suggests he may have written most of it. He certainly soon apologized, saying Shakespeare was honest, upright, and a graceful writer.[4]

Greene's managing to write three books while dying became a joke at the time – a 1598 pamphlet shows him writing in his **shroud**.

Dating the plays

Scholars have to work out the most likely date by looking at lots of different evidence. Some evidence tells us the earliest possible date, other evidence the latest possible date, and yet other evidence may suggest a particular date. This evidence includes:

◆ When the play refers to something that happened in the real world. For example, a play that refers to the Spanish Armada must be written after 1588, when the Armada attacked England.

◆ When a part seems to have been written for a particular actor in Shakespeare's company, in which case it must have been written while that actor was with the company.

◆ When we know there was a performance (but it may not have been the first).

◆ It must be before it was first printed or registered.

Comedies

The Two Gentlemen of Verona is a complicated story of love, jealousy, betrayal, and eventual happiness. *The Taming of the Shrew* was a rewrite of an earlier play. The earlier play still exists, so we can see the changes Shakespeare made. This is the sort of job a young playwright might get – improving an old play. *The Comedy of Errors* deals with the confusions created by two sets of identical twins; one set were masters and the other, servants. It was based on a Roman play by Plautus, which Shakespeare probably studied at school. Shakespeare added the twin servants to increase the confusion.

Histories

The three plays about Henry VI were box office successes. Shakespeare was the main author, but, as was common at the time, he collaborated with other writers. Shakespeare first wrote what we call *Part 2*, then *Part 3* as a sequel, and finally *Part 1* as a prequel. New plays were often only performed three or four times, but *Part 1* was performed 15 times at the Rose between 3 March and 19 June 1592.[5] It was an enormous success. Over 30,000 people, equivalent to 15 per cent of the population of London, came to see it.[6]

Tragedies

Titus Andronicus is thought to be Shakespeare's first tragedy. *Titus Andronicus* has great moments of poetry, and of tension-relieving comedy, but it is driven by acts of brutality and revenge in a three-way quarrel between Titus and his family, the Emperor, and Tamora, queen of the Goths. Modern audiences often see similarities with the films of directors like Quentin Tarantino. During the play (offstage), Titus' daughter, Lavinia, is raped and has her hands and tongue cut off to stop her naming Tamora's sons, Chiron and Demetrius, as her attackers. Titus has his right hand cut off (onstage), and also onstage Chiron and Demetrius have their throats cut. Offstage they are then butchered and baked in a pie, which (onstage) their mother is tricked into eating. In a final onstage frenzy, Titus kills Lavinia (out of pity) and then Tamora (for revenge), before he is killed by the Emperor, who in turn is killed by Titus' son, Lucius.

FACTS

By 1594, Shakespeare had probably written:

The Two Gentlemen of Verona

The Taming of the Shrew

Henry VI Part 2

Henry VI Part 3

Henry VI Part 1

Titus Andronicus

The Comedy of Errors

Special effects in Shakespeare's time were spectacular and gory, with real sheep's blood often used, although without modern detergents they had to be careful with their expensive costumes. Onstage they used pigs' bladders of blood or sponges soaked in blood. In the revival of *Titus* at Shakespeare's Globe (2006), the combination of the horror of the story and the gory effects made up to 30 audience members faint or need to leave each performance!

Titus Andronicus is considered Shakespeare's bloodiest and most violent play.

Opposition to the theatre

We've seen that the Lord Mayor and the rest of the administration of London tried to stop the actors performing plays, but why? There was more than one reason.

- Some thought plays were immoral, and encouraged people to sin, both because of the stories and because of the people they met at playhouses.
- Puritans and other churchmen were worried about plays as a rival attraction to religion. One said (in a sermon), "Wyll not a fylthye playe wyth a blast of a Trumpette, sooner call thyther a thousande, than an houres tolling of a Bell, bring to a sermon a hundred?"[7] Performances on Sundays and holidays (which were still "holy" days) were the most contentious.
- Large numbers of people meeting together might make it easier for Roman Catholic plotters to meet and pass messages.
- The administration worried about "honesty in manners" – they thought going to a play was a big step on the road to illicit sex, drunkenness, and gambling.
- The poor would spend money they could not afford. Perhaps more to the point for the businessmen who ran the city, they might go to a play when they should be working.
- Finally, there was the threat of plague. They didn't know what caused it, but they did know it was highly contagious, and two or three thousand people crushed together at a play seemed likely to spread it.

The theatres close

London suffered small outbreaks of plague in many summers. The outbreak of 1592–1594 was particularly serious, with one contemporary estimating that more than 10,000 died during 1593.[8] The theatres were closed, with only a couple of brief exceptions, from 23 June 1592 to June 1594. The playing companies toured, and struggled to survive. Shakespeare was a writer as well as an actor; what could he do?

SHAKESPEARE'S WORLD EXPLAINED

Bubonic plague

Death from plague was fast and painful. You got a headache, then lethargy, vomiting, aching joints, swellings in the groin, underarms, or neck, a temperature, and sweating. Some survived, but most died in three or four days. As they didn't know what caused it, Elizabethans had no useful treatments.

There were several outbreaks of the Bubonic Plague in Europe from the 14th to the 17th centuries.

How did writers make money?

The modern system of copyright and the idea of intellectual property didn't exist in the 16th century. If Shakespeare wrote a play, he sold it to the acting company, and then they owned it. As a playwright, he didn't get money for every performance; he just got a lump sum at the start (and in the 1590s, this was probably £5). If that play was later published, he wouldn't get any more money at all. Sometimes we think the publisher just got hold of the text and printed and sold it. Other times, the acting company would sell the publisher the text to print, and they would get the money. The same system worked for other books. Men like Robert Greene (see page 27) would write a short book and sell it to a publisher for a pound or two.

Greene died in poverty. It was difficult to make a good living writing pamphlets or plays, but there was another way for a writer to make money – patronage. "Respectable" books, like poetry or history books, could be dedicated to a rich and famous man or woman. Sometimes writers did this in the hope of attracting the attention of a possible patron. Other times, it was repayment because the patron had previously given the writer money, somewhere to live, or both.

What did Shakespeare do?

With the London theatres closed, Shakespeare had a problem. Acting and writing plays were his main ways of making money. Acting was much less well paid when touring the country than in London, and the market for new plays was as dead as many plague-killed Londoners. So he turned his hand to poetry and looked for a patron.

His first long poem, *Venus and Adonis*, was published in February 1593. Based on a classical story in Ovid's *Metamorphoses*, a book Shakespeare would have studied at school, it tells of the love of the goddess Venus for Adonis, a beautiful young man. In Ovid, who wrote the story in 75 lines, Adonis returns her love. In Shakespeare's version, there is much more tension as Adonis rejects her love and tries to avoid her. Shakespeare's story is longer, too – he wrote 1194 lines. It is a very erotic poem, and was Shakespeare's only real bestseller during his lifetime.

TO THE RIGHT
HONOVRABLE, HENRY
VVriothefley, Earle of Southhampton,
and Baron of Titchfield.

HE loue I dedicate to your Lordfhip is without end: wherof this Pamphlet without beginning is but a fuperfluous Moity. The warrant I haue of your Honourable difpofition, not the worth of my vntutord Lines makes it affured of acceptance. VVhat I haue done is yours, what I haue to doe is yours, being part in all I haue, deuoted yours. VVere my worth greater, my duety would fhew greater, meane time, as it is, it is bound to your Lordfhip; To whom I wifh long life ftill lengthned with all happineffe.

Your Lordfhips in all duety.

William Shakefpeare.

A 2

The dedication to the Earl of Southampton from *The Rape of Lucrece*. We only have two letters written by Shakespeare, this one, and the dedication to *Venus and Adonis*, and both were really for publication. For modern taste, it is a little over the top in the compliments it pays.

Shakespeare's second long poem, *The Rape of Lucrece*, published in May 1594, is darker. This time it is about lust, not love, and Lucrece, after being raped, kills herself. Both poems were dedicated to Henry Wriothesley (pronounced "Risley"), 3rd Earl of Southampton. Most scholars think the *Lucrece* dedication suggests, when compared to the *Venus* one, that Shakespeare knew Southampton better, and may have received some patronage from him.

Back to the theatre

In the summer of 1594, the plague was over, and the theatres were open again. The Lord Chamberlain had a plan. He was the courtier responsible for Queen Elizabeth's entertainment, and he was looking for a solution to the quarrelling between the City and the Privy Council over plays in London. He came up with a new scheme. Only two companies would be allowed – his, and the Lord Admiral's. There would be no playing inside London, but his company would have the Theatre, north of the city, and the Admiral's would have the Rose, south of the Thames. The existing plays, and the best actors, seem to have been divided up as well.

Shakespeare joined the Lord Chamberlain's Men, and they started performing at the Newington Butts theatre on 3 June.[9] Two days later, they played *Titus Andronicus*. Soon they moved on to the Theatre. Shakespeare became a **sharer** in the company. The sharers ran the company and took the profits. Normally a sharer had to buy his share, so Shakespeare presumably had enough money to do this. At Christmas 1594, the company performed for the Queen, and in March the next year, Shakespeare, as a sharer, was one of the men who collected the money when they eventually got paid.

The acting company normally took all the entrance money paid by people standing in the yard, and half of the extra money paid by those in the galleries. Out of their income, the company would buy the costumes and the plays, and pay the actors and other staff. The profits, of course, were divided between the sharers.

What makes Shakespeare different?

We've seen Shakespeare was known as a playwright in 1594. Soon, he was known as a master playwright. In a small section of a 666-page book, *Palladis Tamia, Wits Treasury*, entered on the Stationers' Register on 7 September 1598, Francis Meres wrote a chapter comparing the leading authors of his day to the great Roman and Greek writers:

> *the sweete wittie soule of Ovid lives in mellifluous and hony-tongued Shakespeare, witnes his Venus and Adonis, his Lucrece, his sugred Sonnets among his private friends, etc. As Plautus and Seneca are accounted the best for Comedy and Tragedy among the Latines: so Shakespeare among the English is the most excellent in both kinds for the stage; for Comedy, witnes his* Gentlemen of Verona, *his* Errors, *his* Love labors lost, *his* Love labours wonne, *his* Midsummer night dreame, & *his* Merchant of Venice: *for Tragedy his* Richard the 2. Richard the 3. Henry the 4. King John, Titus Andronicus *and his* Romeo and Juliet.... *I say that the* **Muses** *would speak with Shakespeares fine filed phrase, if they would speake English.*[1]

What made Shakespeare different from other playwrights at the time is a big part of what made him so successful so quickly. It came:
- partly from the insights he got as an actor,
- partly from his skill as a writer and his profound empathy, and
- partly from his secure position as a sharer in his company and (as we will see later) part-owner of a theatre.

Shakespeare as an actor

Modern actors often say how well Shakespeare's text works on the stage. His experience as an actor was a great help to him as a writer. Cast lists from his time have not survived, but, when some plays were printed, they had a list of the actors, but not the parts they played. The *First Folio* lists Shakespeare as an actor in his own plays. He is listed twice in plays by Ben Jonson, as a comedian in *Every Man in His Humour* (1598) and as a tragedian in *Sejanus* (1603). So he acted throughout this period – but what parts did he play? The only contemporary reference is a poem by John Davies, from 1610, which said

Here Richard III (Mark Rylance) suggests that Lady Anne (Johnny Flynn) should kill him if she will not accept him as a lover. This was an **original practices** production of *Richard III* at Shakespeare's Globe in 2012.

Shakespeare played "Kingly parts". Later tradition suggests he played the Ghost in Hamlet, but this was first written down over 90 years after he died.

Shakespeare the celebrity

A Londoner's diary for 13 March 1602 tells a story about Shakespeare and Richard Burbage, a leading actor. A woman was so taken with Burbage as Richard III that she wanted to meet him after the show. Shakespeare overheard the plan, and turned up first. When Burbage arrived, saying, "Richard III is at the door", Shakespeare's called down, "William the Conqueror was before Richard III". The story may or may not be true. It is the sort of celebrity gossip common today and shows us Shakespeare and Burbage were celebrities in their day.[2]

FACTS

Between 1594 and 1603 Shakespeare probably wrote:

Richard III
Love's Labour's Lost
Richard II
Romeo and Juliet
A Midsummer Night's Dream
King John
The Merchant of Venice
Henry IV Part 1
The Merry Wives of Windsor
Henry IV Part 2
Much Ado About Nothing
Henry V
Julius Caesar
As You Like It
Hamlet
Twelfth Night
Troilus and Cressida

Shakespeare as a writer

Shakespeare's craft as a writer developed between 1594 and 1603. The characters in the plays he wrote at this time have more depth. They tell the audience about their motives and hopes in **soliloquies**. The themes become more serious. For example, in the two *Henry IV* plays, the audience is asked to think about issues like the relationship between fathers and sons, guilt, ambition, and the effects of politics on the lives of normal citizens. Shakespeare also started to use humour in a new way. The *Henry IV* plays have a comic sub-plot, but Shakespeare discovered a way to make these comic scenes develop the themes, and to make the characters like Falstaff full of the contradictions we find in real people (see page 38).

The sonnets

Shakespeare published a series of 154 poems called **sonnets** in 1609. He wrote at least 103 of them in the late 1590s. We know Francis Meres had read some by 1598, and two were printed in a pirate edition in 1599. This is more proof of Shakespeare's growing reputation – it was worth the publisher's risk to pirate some Shakespeare poems because they would sell well.

The sonnets are a great temptation to a biographer, because they could be looked at as autobiographical. They tell a story of the growing love between the poet and a young man, also his love and lust (mixed with guilt and shame) for someone referred to as his dark mistress, and then his despair when he discovers the mistress and the young man are also lovers.

Scholars have used forests of paper arguing that they have identified the other two real people in this love triangle. Candidates for the youth include the earls of Southampton and Pembroke, and for the dark lady, they range from Lucy Negro, a well-known prostitute, to the poet Emilia Lanier.[3] None of these theories is completely convincing, and the sonnets may not be autobiographical at all. Shakespeare may have developed the story to make the poems more interesting. Empathy – the ability to imagine another person's life from the inside – is one of his great skills.

The sonnets do show us an important part of Shakespeare's craft as a writer. Comparing the two printed in the pirate edition in 1599 with the 1609 "official" versions shows small changes, which add up to a great improvement. He was a reviser. He could come back to his work and make it better. Indeed, in the plays, he rarely bothers to invent his own stories: he takes existing ones, changes them, and makes them better.

A Shakespeare manuscript

In the *First Folio*, the actors Heminges and Condell say Shakespeare wrote fluently: "what he thought, he uttered with that easinesse, that wee have scarse received from him a blot in his papers". This is the only surviving play manuscript, we think, in Shakespeare's handwriting. It isn't a play we normally think of as by Shakespeare. It comes from *Sir Thomas More*, a multi-author play with one Shakespeare scene, where More stops an anti-immigrant riot in London. It shows some crossing out, but his writing does seem to have flowed. The last couple of lines read:

> *That breaking out in hidious violence*
> *Would not aford you an abode on earth*

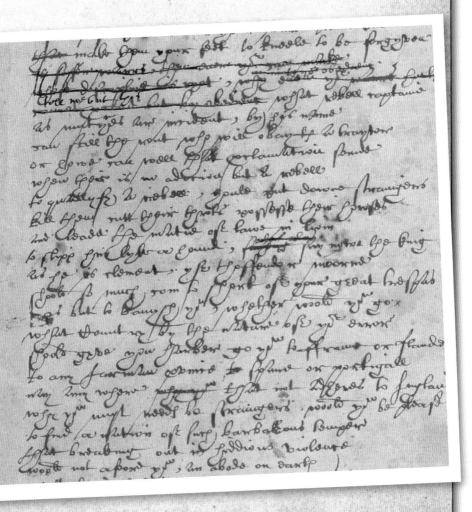

Falstaff (Roger Allam) keeps a modern audience spellbound, in *Henry IV Part 2*, at Shakespeare's Globe in 2010.

Falstaff

In the *Henry IV* plays, Sir John Falstaff is a drunkard, a liar, and a thief. He spends most of his time with criminals and prostitutes, and some of it with the future Henry V. Shakespeare makes him full of contradictions, and a compelling character at the heart of the play. But Shakespeare didn't call him Falstaff. Shakespeare originally called him Oldcastle, the name of a real knight in Henry IV's reign. Shakespeare's company performed *Henry IV Part 1* at court over Christmas 1596. It was a great success, but not with Lord Cobham, the new Lord Chamberlain. Oldcastle was one of his ancestors, and he was outraged. Shakespeare was a famous and successful actor and playwright then,

FACTS

Francis Meres' list of plays by Shakespeare includes *Love's Labour's Won*. This is a mystery. It could be a different title for a surviving play – it fits *The Taming of The Shrew* – or it could have been a sequel to *Love's Labour's Lost*, which seems to end in the middle of the story. A play with this title was printed, and it is on a list of a bookseller's stock in 1603. No copy has been found – yet.[4]

and has become world famous since. But in 1596, he was nowhere near as important as Lord Cobham. Shakespeare changed the name to Falstaff, and in the epilogue to *Henry IV Part 2*, he apologized:

> our humble author will continue
> the story, with Sir John in it,
> and make you merry with fair
> Katherine of Fraunce, where (for
> anything I know) Falstaffe shall
> die of a sweat, unless already a
> be killed with your hard opinions.
> For Olde-castle dyed a martyre,
> and this is not the man.[5]

Deaths in the family

Many scholars think Shakespeare's work gets darker in the late 1590s. In August 1596, his 11-year old son, Hamnet, died in Stratford. We don't know why he died, nor whether Shakespeare was in Stratford or in London then. We may see his grief in the lines he wrote that year in *King John*, as Lady Constance mourns her son: "Grief fills the room up of my absent child: | Lies in his bed, walks up and down with me".[6] But it can be dangerous for a biographer to use the plays in this way. These lines come in a passage where Constance is criticized for showing too much grief.

Less unexpectedly, Shakespeare's father, John, died in his seventies in September 1601.

 Myth Shakespeare wrote alone

Over 50 per cent of Elizabethan and **Jacobean** plays were collaborations between two or more playwrights. Shakespeare mainly wrote alone, but he also collaborated with other writers. An early collaboration is *Henry VI Part 1* (collaborator unknown). At the end of his career, he wrote with John Fletcher (who succeeded him as the company's playwright). Together they wrote three plays: *Henry VIII*, *The Two Noble Kinsmen*, and *Cardenio*. Only *Henry VIII* is in the *First Folio*, and the text of *Cardenio* has not survived. Scholars think he also worked with other writers in *Timon of Athens*, *All's Well That Ends Well*, and *Pericles*. Then there are plays like *Sir Thomas More* and *Edward III*, where Shakespeare wrote a scene or two in a multi-author play.[7]

Myth Queen Elizabeth and *Merry Wives of Windsor*

There is a myth that Queen Elizabeth enjoyed Falstaff so much that she demanded a new play where Falstaff is in love (*Merry Wives of Windsor*). She gave Shakespeare two weeks to get it ready, so she could see it. The truth is that this tale was first printed in 1702, over 100 years later, and it was linked to a new performance of the play. It is unlikely to be true.

Problems with playhouses

The Lord Chamberlain's Men were playing in the Theatre in late 1596. James Burbage owned it, and his son Richard was the star actor in the company. However, James only leased the land, and the **lease** ended on 25 March 1597. James died early in 1597, and the lease passed to his son Cuthbert. The landlord, Giles Allen, wanted the land back, and would not renew the lease. The company played on at the Theatre for a few months, then moved to the nearby Curtain.[8]

Both the Theatre (opened 1576) and the Curtain (opened by December 1577) were old playhouses, smaller than the newer Rose and Swan theatres, which were south of the river on Bankside. James Burbage had planned to move the company to a new indoor playhouse, in what had been part of the Blackfriars monastery, which he bought and fitted out. This plan failed because the other residents of the Blackfriars got the Privy Council to ban the planned theatre.

This photo shows the building of the modern Globe, which opened on Bankside in 1997. It is a reconstruction of the original theatre made as accurately as possible. The framework of structural timbers take the weight of the structure, and the gaps are then filled in with lath and plaster, and doors and windows. Go to page 43 to see the finished theatre.

Both the Burbage brothers and the Lord Chamberlain's Men were in trouble. Cuthbert and Richard Burbage had little or no money – James had spent it all on the failed Blackfriars plan. With the company at the Curtain, the Burbages weren't getting the theatre owner's share of the takings. The Curtain was an old and small theatre, which was bad for the company, too. The solution was appropriately dramatic. The Burbages would raise some money, take down the Theatre building, and use its timbers to make a new and better theatre on Bankside.

Building the Globe

First, they had to raise the money. The system of running the Lord Chamberlain's Men by sharers was working, so they extended it to the ownership of the new theatre. The Burbages created ten shares, kept five, and offered one each to Shakespeare and four other actors. These shareowners were called **housekeepers**.

Theatre on the move

The Theatre lease that Burbage had with Allen said Burbage owned, and could take down, anything he built on the land – and he had built the Theatre. So on 28 December, during a snowy night, the Burbages, with a gang of actors, builders, and some hired muscle, turned up and started taking the Theatre down. It would have taken several days. Timber-framed buildings work a bit like flatpack furniture. The carpenter made the framework in his yard, then took it apart, transported to the site, and re-erected it. You can see the frame clearly in the photo of the reconstructed Globe. Taking the structural timbers down meant they could be reused in a different building. Builders in the 16th century often did this, and this time they used the timbers to build the Globe Theatre, which opened in 1599.

Businessman

Shakespeare was now a businessman as well as an actor and a playwright. He was part-owner of the Globe, London's newest, largest, and grandest theatre. It was also a theatre built by actors for actors. Actors made all the decisions about how big the stage should be and what the sightlines would be. A German tourist described a visit to the Globe on 21 September 1599:

> After dinner, about two o'clock, I went with my companions over the water, and in the thatched [play]house, we saw the tragedy of the first Emperor Julius Caesar, very well acted, with at least 15 characters. At the end of the play, they danced together admirably and exceedingly gracefully, according to their custom, two in each group dressed in men's and two in women's clothes.[10]

He had been to Shakespeare's *Julius Caesar*. Shakespeare had been paid for writing the play, he got a share of the acting company's profits from the performance, and he got a share of the theatre owner's profits, too. This means two things. First, Shakespeare the businessman was starting to make money – and in the next chapter we'll look at what he did with it. Second, it also means that Shakespeare the writer had more freedom. He didn't have to keep banging out more plays to make a living. He could afford to take more time, and more care, than other playwrights.

Treason!

The last years of Elizabeth's reign were difficult. Harvests were bad, food was expensive, and some people starved. Elizabeth had no children, and discussion about who should be the next monarch was forbidden. In 1601, the Earl of Essex, once Elizabeth's **favourite**, but now under house arrest, planned a rebellion. His supporters included the Earl of Southampton, who earlier was probably Shakespeare's patron. Some of the rebels approached the Lord Chamberlain's Men and asked them to perform Shakespeare's *Richard II* at the Globe on 7 February. In the play, Richard is forced to **abdicate**, and Henry IV takes the throne. The plotters hoped it would put Londoners in the mood for a revolt. They were wrong, and Essex's rebellion the next day was easily squashed.

Rebuilding the Globe

Shakespeare's Globe, as it is called, was the idea of Sam Wanamaker, an American actor and director. He spent over 20 years raising the money, and died before it was finished. Scholars played a key part, collecting all the possible evidence about the size and shape of the original Globe theatre. However, this was very inconclusive. They had to make many inferences, just as we do in looking at Shakespeare's life, and the resulting building is as accurate as it can be, and must be very like the original.

The Lord Chamberlain's Men were in trouble. The government didn't believe in coincidences and wanted an explanation for the performance of *Richard II*. It summoned one of the sharers to explain. A group of men, he said, wanted to see the play, and asked them to put it on that Saturday. The actors didn't like the idea, saying it was an old play and they would get a poor crowd. The men offered them £2 to do it, on top of the money they took at the box office. They weren't traitors, just businessmen who took a good deal. They were forgiven, and played for the Queen the night before Essex's execution.[11]

Shakespeare had survived a difficult moment. When the Queen died, in 1603, he was a successful man, but what would happen next?

FACTS

Christmas 1596 *Henry IV Part 1* performed at court.
7 September 1598 Francis Meres praises Shakespeare's poems and plays.
1599 Two Shakespeare sonnets are printed in a pirate edition.
Summer 1599 The Globe Theatre opens with Shakespeare as a shareholder.

Was Shakespeare rich?

People have been interested in whether Shakespeare was rich, since soon after he died. Forty-five years later, John Ward, then vicar of Stratford, wrote Shakespeare had "an allowance so large hee spent att the Rate of £1000 a year as I have heard".[1] To spend £1,000 a year would mean he was very wealthy, but is this true or a myth? We might say great show business entrepreneurs today (like Andrew Lloyd Webber) are rich, but Shakespeare lived in a very **hierarchical** society. To make sense of this question in his world, we have to answer two questions: was he moving upwards in the class system, and did he have a lot of money? If he did, was it anything like £1,000 a year?

William Shakespeare, gentleman

We've seen that Shakespeare was the son of a small-town trader, and that his father, John, grew in prosperity and then hit hard times. John had approached the College of Arms about being recognized as a gentleman, but dropped the scheme when his business was in trouble.

What did it mean to be a gentleman? The answer is simple: it meant a step up the social hierarchy. A gentleman had a coat of arms and higher status. Even in 1597, it was looking back to medieval times, where bearing arms meant both having a coat of arms and being able to raise and equip soldiers to fight for the monarch.

SHAKESPEARE'S WORLD EXPLAINED

The College of Arms
The College of Arms still exists. As in Shakespeare's day, it grants coats of arms. The College is a group of officials called heralds with rather grand medieval titles, such as "Garter King of Arms", "Portcullis Pursuivant", and "York Herald". It is still on the site Shakespeare went to near St Paul's Cathedral. The building Shakespeare visited burned down in the Great Fire of London (1666), and was rebuilt. The heralds saved all the records, and they include the original notes for the Shakespeare application.

In 1596, the Shakespeares went back to the Garter King of Arms, a herald at the College of Arms. The application was in John's name – it had to be, as he was the "head" of the family. But scholars assume it was handled by William – a successful man based in London. If it was William, then he was successful in this, too. The Shakespeares got their coat of arms, and the status of gentlemen. William was proud. In all legal documents after the grant, he signs himself "William Shakespeare, gentleman".[2]

There was a problem in 1602. Another herald complained the Garter King of Arms had been granting coats of arms to inappropriate people, and one of his examples was "Shakespear the Player".[3] Calling Shakespeare a player (actor) was a deliberate attempt to make him sound unworthy. Players were often listed with vagabonds and **sturdy beggars** in Elizabethan law. However, the grant of arms to the Shakespeares was upheld. One thing we do learn from the complaint is it still made sense to call Shakespeare an actor in 1602.

The Shakespeare coat of arms is on the monument in the church in Stratford put up by William Shakespeare's family immediately after his death. Putting it on his monument suggests they were proud to have been granted a coat of arms.

We have the answer to the first part of our enquiry. Shakespeare was rising up the social scale.

This is the only picture of New Place. George Vertue visited Stratford in 1737, over 100 years after Shakespeare died. He made this sketch later, from memory.

Man of property

We know Shakespeare was living in London in 1597, just inside the old city wall, a short walk from the Theatre and the Curtain playhouses. He was either renting a house or living as a lodger in somebody else's. By 1599, he had moved south of the river, near the Globe. Later, in the early 1600s, he was living as a lodger in a house back north of the river in Silver Street. But when he wanted to buy a house, and to invest in property, he didn't think about London – he thought about Stratford.

We assume, but we don't know, that Anne and their children always lived with William's parents in the family home in Stratford, When William decided to buy a house in 1597, it was in Stratford. The deeds say he paid £60 for New Place, which was the second largest house in the town. He probably paid much more. People kept the price down in official documents to keep their tax bills low, and then made a secret extra payment. This was the house a successful man would buy, and Shakespeare probably spent more money improving it. He sold a load of stone to the Council in 1598, which we assume was left over from building work.

New Place had extensive gardens, and Shakespeare enlarged them, buying land at the end of his garden, and knocking down a cottage. It had two gardens, two barns, and two orchards. The house itself was large. A survey 47 years after Shakespeare died said it had 10 fireplaces – which means it had more than 10 rooms. The site of the house and gardens can still be seen in Stratford.

In England, in Shakespeare's time and for hundreds of years after, if you made money from "trade", you then invested it in land. This gave a steady income and was respectable. This is exactly what Shakespeare did.

In 1602, he bought 127 acres of arable land, plus grazing rights on common land for £320. In the English Midlands in 2013, arable land sold for around £7,500 an acre. At today's prices this land and grazing would cost just over £1 million.[4] This doesn't mean Shakespeare became a farmer. He probably rented out the land; this is how a gentleman was supposed to live – on his rents.

Shakespeare's property dealings show he was a wealthy man and one who was investing his money carefully and conventionally.

SHAKESPEARE'S WORLD EXPLAINED

Money then and now

In the 400-plus years since Shakespeare bought New Place, the value British people give to property has changed. Part of the reason is supply and demand. In 1600, the population of England was perhaps 4 million, whereas it was nearly 53 million in 2011. There was plenty of space in 1600, even in towns. Now 10 times as many people fit in the same area. Today, New Place might cost £1.75 million.

Businessman and investor

Some people have accused Shakespeare of being a tax dodger, a hoarder, and a **usurer**. They say that a great poet and playwright would be too sensitive to behave in this grasping way. The records do show us that Shakespeare was careful with money, and was concerned to make sure his family wasn't hit by poverty, as it was when he was a boy. But was he as greedy about money and uncaring about people as has been suggested?

We know he was twice late paying his taxes – perhaps only paying his 1597 and 1598 taxes in 1601.[5] The records about non-payment of tax also tell us where he was living in those years (see page 46). These aren't the only years when tax records survive, and since these are the only years he is listed as not paying, he probably usually paid on time. So for the charge of tax-dodger, the answer is *not (very) guilty*.

Shakespeare is sometimes accused of being a hoarder and a usurer. Today, being a "hoarder" is what we might call being a "speculator". When there was a shortage of goods, such as grain and malt, hoarders bought, waited for the price to go up, and then sold at a high profit. In 1598, to stop people hoarding, the government ordered a census of all holdings of grain and malt. Shakespeare had 80 bushels of malt in his barn. Some would have been for the household's own brewing. We do know he later sold malt, so he may have been doing some speculating, but not on a large scale – he only had the third largest holding in his own street. We also know he sold malt on credit in 1604, and loaned money to neighbours and business partners. He twice sued for the non-payment of debts. So for these charges, the verdict must be *a bit guilty*.[6]

Shakespeare's biggest investment was in tithes. Simply, a tithe was a charge of a tenth of the value of income – in this case, the income from farming land. These tithes were the way the church was financed. The church sold the right to collect some tithes around Stratford for 92 years, to raise some capital. Shakespeare bought into the last 31 years of this lease for £440. The tithes gave him a profit of £60 a year.[7] So the investment would take 8 years to get back its cost, and would then make profits for 23 years (eventually a total profit of £1,420, or 323 per cent.). This is another cautious investment, like land. If he was serious about being a moneylender, and charged the maximum legal interest rate of 10 per cent a year, he could have made much more by lending out the £440 pounds, than by buying the tithes.

Tax records

Taxes were based on the value of your possessions. The valuations were not very accurate. Richard Burbage, star actor and fellow shareholder in the Globe and the Lord Chamberlain's Men, had his goods valued at £3 in the same assessment as Shakespeare's were valued at £5.

A cautious investor

These transactions show us Shakespeare took good care of his money. He was a rich man, with a rich man's house and investments. But he wasn't fabulously wealthy, like a great aristocrat. He was transferring the money he made from the theatre to property, land, and tithes. The theatre might not be safe in the long term. Plague could shut theatres for a year or two, or the Puritans could get them closed for good. Shakespeare wasn't a gambler; he chose safe and respectable investments, acting like a typical country gentleman. And he had become a gentleman, if not a typical one.

At the start of this chapter, we saw a later vicar of Stratford estimate Shakespeare spent £1,000 a year. We can now see that this is myth, not reality. The income he needed to make these investments was probably only £300–£400 a year.

FACTS

15 November 1597 Listed as not having paid his taxes (5 shillings) in St Helen's parish, London.

4 February 1598 At a time of malt and grain shortage, listed as having 80 bushels of malt in Stratford.

1 October 1598 Listed as not having paid his next tax bill (13 shillings, 4 pence) in St Helen's parish.

25 October 1598 Soon after this date, probably lent Richard Quiney £30.

1599 A list of unpaid taxes for St Helen's parish says he has moved to Bankside.

1601 Shakespeare's back taxes probably paid.

1604 Sold Philip Rogers, an apothecary in Stratford, 20 bushels of malt worth £2 on credit.

24 July 1605 Buys a half interest in tithes for £440.

17 August 1608 Sues Richard Addenbroke of Stratford for a debt of £6 plus £14 shillings damages.

The King's man

Shakespeare's company performed before Queen Elizabeth for the last time on 2 February 1603. By this point, she was old and sick. In March, she fell ill, refused to go to bed, and sat in a chair day and night. She refused food, and refused to be treated by her doctors. Elizabeth died on 24 March. Until the last day of her life, she refused to say who should rule after her death. But Sir Robert Cecil said that on the last day she whispered to him that it should be her cousin, James VI of Scotland.

James was 37 when he became James I of England. He was a successful king of Scotland, and a well-read and intelligent man. On the other hand, he had some odd characteristics – he usually wore heavily padded **doublets** because he was scared of being stabbed, his tongue was said to be too big for his mouth, and he sometimes got very drunk at public feasts. As King of Scotland, he had always been short of money, and England seemed a very rich country to him. He was generous, giving lavish gifts to his favourites.

His generosity continued. Ten days after reaching London, he issued an order for the Lord Chamberlain's Men to become his own troupe of players – the King's Men. A **royal patent** quickly followed:

> lawrence ffletcher, William Shakespeare, Richard Burbage, Augustine Phillippes, John Heminges, Henrie Condell, [three others] and the rest of theire Assosiates freely to use and exercise the Arte and faculty of playinge Comedies Tragedies histories Enterludes moralls pastoralls Stage plaies and suche others like as theie have alreadie studied or hereafter shall use or studie aswell for the recreation of our lovinge Subjectes as for our Solace and pleasure when wee shall thincke good to see them duringe our pleasure. And ... to shewe and exercise publiquely to theire best Commoditie when the infection of the plague shall decrease aswell within their nowe usual howse called the Globe within our County of Surrey as also within anie towne halls or Moute halls or other conveniente places within the liberties and freedome of anie Cittie universittie towne or Boroughe whatsoever within our said Realmes and dominions.[1]

Did it make any difference?

This is a powerful document. It gives the company the King's patronage, and when they needed to tour, they could say that the king wanted them to be able to play in any town, borough, or university – a powerful encouragement to local councils not to send them away.

We can learn from it as well. There were three main acting companies in London in 1603. Shakespeare's must have been the most successful, because they got the King's patronage. The other companies became the Queen's Men and the Prince's Men.

King James VI and I (c. 1606) was painted about three years after he became King of England.

In the last 10 years of Elizabeth's reign, Shakespeare's company played at court 32 times, an average of just over three times a year. In the first 10 years of James' reign, the company played at court 138 times, an average of just under 14 times a year. So as the King's Men, and with a king who wanted to see more plays, they played at court much more often.

They didn't just act in plays for the king. The sharers had the rank of "Grooms of the Chamber", and as such, they were issued with 4½ yards of red cloth to make their official clothes. They needed them to wear when they took part in the King's coronation procession in March 1604.[2] They probably also wore them when they were used as special attendants to wait on the Spanish Ambassador, who was in England in August that year to sign a peace treaty. Presumably they were chosen because they were imposing-looking men, who knew how to behave (and act). Shakespeare had come a long way – from a glover's shop in Stratford to being a servant of the King.

Royal records

The King's Men will have kept careful records, but they have not survived. The royal court, on the other hand, kept records that have survived, so more is known about performances at court than about those at the Globe. Opposite is a page from the accounts of the Revels Office, which arranged for plays to be seen by the king and the court. It is divided into three columns. The first column lists the company of actors, "The plaiers". The middle column gives the date and the play. The third column is headed "The poets", the term used for playwrights. The third entry up from the bottom reads:

By his Ma[tis]   *On Shrousunday A play of the*   *Shaxberd*
plaiers: -   *Marthant of Venis*

His Majesty's Players means the King's Men. The day is **Shrove** Sunday, and the play *The Merchant of Venice*. Shaxberd is one of the more unusual spellings of Shakespeare. Shrovetide was a three-day festival before the beginning of Lent, with plays each day. On Shrove Tuesday (two days later), we have *The Martchant of Venis Againe Commanded By the Kings Ma[tie]*. King James enjoyed the play so much, he insisted on a second performance. Almost certainly, another play aleady would have been booked for that day, perhaps from another company.

Records like these can be hard to read. The odd spelling may show the clerk spoke with a Scots accent, but it isn't only the spelling that is different. Handwriting has changed since 1605, too. Look at the third entry from the bottom and compare it with the transcript above.

- *s* can be written as it is now, or as a long stroke with a tail below the line (*Srousunday*)
- *t* may not be crossed, and *h* has a curled tail below the line and *e* can look like a modern *r* (*the*)
- *V* can look like *u* (*Venis*)
- when *n m i* are written together you just get a series of down strokes, joined at the top – these are called minims – (*Venis*).

Can you find another play that could be by Shakespeare? (A clue: it doesn't have *Shaxberd* in the poet column.)

The plaiers	On Twelfe Night	The poets
	wch maskes & mowtes wth eleven Laydies of the Lomde to Accumpayney: for ma no Hamy in great shoues off Deuised wth A Last In wch Excelent Musike	
By his Ma^tis plaiers:	On the: 7: off January was played the play off Henry the fift:	
By his ma^tis plaiers:-	The: 8: off January: A play Cauled Euery on out of his vmor	
By his Ma^tis plaiers:	On Candelmas night A playe Euery one Jn his vmor	
	The Sunday following A playe probited And disscharged	
By his ma^tis plaiers:	On Shrousunday A play off the Marthant of veins	Shaxberd
By his ma^tis plaiers:-	On Shroumonday A Tragide of The Spanishe Maz:	
By his ma^tie plaiers:-	On Shroutusday A play Cauled The Marthant of Venis Againe Comanded By the Kings Matie	Shaxberd:

A lodger in Silver Street

In 1604, in London, Shakespeare lived in the house of the Mountjoys in Silver Street, north of the river, just inside London's old city walls. They were French Protestant refugees, working in the fashion industry, making expensive women's hats called tires. It was a quiet area of London, north of the bustle of Cheapside, the main shopping street, and west of Wood Street, a main road out of the city through Cripplegate. To walk to the Globe would take just over half an hour, crossing the river at London Bridge.

We know Shakespeare lived with the Mountjoys, because some events in 1604 finished up as a court case in 1612. Shakespeare testified in the case, and his testimony, written down by the clerk, is the only record we have of anything he said. The court case concerns the marriage of Stephen Belott, the Mountjoys' former apprentice (who lived with and worked for them) and Mary, their only child. There was talk of a marriage, but nothing was settled. Shakespeare was asked by Mrs Mountjoy to "move and perswade" Belott to marry Mary, and he did "move and perswade [him] thereunto".

The issue in court was Mary's dowry. Belott claimed he was promised £60, and £200 in Mountjoy's will. Asked by another witness, earlier in the quarrel, Shakespeare said it was "ffyftye poundes in money and Certain Househould stuffe", but when it came to court he changed his mind – by then he "rememberithe not, nor knoweth" about the £200.[3]

What should we make of this? Was Shakespeare getting old and forgetful? He was 40 in 1604, and 48 when he testified in court. Did he change his story, or was the other witness making a false claim? As so often, even when we have evidence, we have more questions than answers.

Another man involved in the court case was George Wilkins. Wilkins was an unsavoury character, who seems to have run a brothel, and had convictions for violence, often against prostitutes. He had a short career as a writer, and he and Shakespeare collaborated on *Pericles* in 1607 or 1608.

Part of a map of London, probably made in the 1560s. The Mountjoy's house is marked in red, on the corner of Muggle Street (blue) and Silver Street (yellow). John Heminges, friend and colleague of Shakespeare in the King's Men, and an editor of the First Folio, lived nearby in Addle Street (green).

Muggle Street   Silver Street

The Mountjoy's house   Addle Street

Playing indoors

Back in 1596, when he was worried about the lease of the Theatre, James Burbage invested in one of the largest indoor spaces in the whole of London, the Parliament Chamber, which had been part of the old Blackfriars monastery. It was called this because Parliament had met there a number of times, most recently in 1523. He converted it into an indoor theatre, but his plans alarmed his new neighbours, who got the Privy Council to ban its use as a professional theatre. James died in 1597, and the conversion costs almost bankrupted his sons, Richard and Cuthbert. In 1600, the Burbage brothers leased the Blackfriars theatre to Henry Evans, who set up a children's company to act there. After producing a number of politically provocative plays, the children's company was banned by order of King James. In 1608, Evans gave the lease back to Richard Burbage.

The Blackfriars Theatre

Now the company was the *King's* Men, it had enough powerful support to be able to use its indoor theatre. The system of shareholders owning the Globe was working well, and the Burbages extended it to the Blackfriars. Shakespeare got a one-seventh share, which, after another housekeeper died, became a one-sixth share. But what was their "new" theatre like?

- It was much smaller than the Globe. From the back wall of the stage to the end of the **auditorium** was 20 metres (66 feet), and it can have been no more than 14 metres (46 feet) wide.
- Unlike the Globe, there were no stage pillars, because the whole building had a roof.
- The stage was smaller than the Globe, but, like the Globe, it did have two side doors plus a central door, or **discovery space**, in the back wall. There was a **stage trap** halfway between the back wall and the front of the stage.
- Like the Globe, **galleries** for the audience to sit in ran round the auditorium, and now they ran along the side of the stage, as you can see in the photo. Fashionable young men (known as gallants), could choose to sit on stools on the stage itself.
- The most significant difference was the lighting. Performances started about 2 p.m., and finished about 5 p.m. There were windows, but 5 p.m. in a London winter is dark, and they used hundreds of candles.

This performance took place in a modern reconstruction of the Blackfriars Playhouse at the American Shakespeare Center, Staunton, Virginia, USA.

A new plan – and more profit

From 1609, the King's Men had a new plan – perform at the Globe in the summer and the Blackfriars in the winter. They normally swapped over in May and October. The Blackfriars only held about 500 people, while the Globe held 3,000; but the prices and profits were higher indoors. Blackfriars had no standing, and the cheapest seats were 6 pence (in the galleries). To sit on the benches in the pit (the equivalent of the yard) cost 1 shilling, to sit on a stool on the stage 2 shillings, and a box in the galleries 2 shillings and 6 pence. We know the company's income from just 10 performances at the Globe and Blackfriars, and the average profit was over double per performance at Blackfriars.

This happened at the end of Shakespeare's career, and he only wrote six plays where he could have been thinking about performing in the new theatre. However, the text for some of his earlier plays was revised for the Blackfriars, as we will see when we look at *Macbeth*.

Did Shakespeare's writing develop?

Shakespeare's plays didn't change overnight when Elizabeth died. The most significant change in his later writing, which started before 1603, is that he tells us less about the motives of major characters. This adds a depth and complexity to the plays. For example, in *King Lear*, the play starts with a "love test" – the king will divide his kingdom between his three daughters, and each must say how much she loves him. Shakespeare took the story from an earlier play, where this is a way to trick the youngest, Cordelia, into marrying the man her father prefers. Shakespeare's Lear doesn't have this motive, and the audience have to work out why for themselves. This makes Lear seem more, not less, human, because in our lives few people act with simple and obvious motives.[4]

FACTS

Between 1603 and 1610 Shakespeare probably wrote:
Measure for Measure
Othello
All's Well That Ends Well
Timon of Athens (with Thomas Middleton)
King Lear
Macbeth
Antony and Cleopatra
Pericles (with George Wilkins)
Coriolanus
The Winter's Tale
Cymbeline

In this scene from the Shakespeare's Globe 2008 production of *King Lear*, Cordelia (Jodie McNee) fails her father's "love test". She says she loves Lear (David Calder), but when she marries, she will love her husband as much.

No single theme unites Shakespeare's plays from 1603, when James became king, to 1610. Some scholars suggest he got ideas and insights from the people he met during these years:

- The Mountjoys and the problems of being an immigrant may have helped when writing *Othello*, who was a black immigrant in Venice.
- George Wilkins, and the seedy world he lived in, may have supplied some ideas for *Measure for Measure*.
- Stephen Belott and Mary Mountjoy may have given him some insights into the problems of a couple where the woman was more in love than the man, which is the central storyline in *All's Well That Ends Well*.

Other scholars suggest he was more concerned with writing plays to please the king:

- *King Lear* shows the dangers of a divided kingdom. (James tried to unite England and Scotland.)
- *Measure for Measure* is about how a ruler should behave.
- *Macbeth* shows one of King James' ancestors as a hero.

There is some truth in both these views, but not enough. Shakespeare was an artist writing about what interested him. He was also a businessman who wrote to please an audience – both in the theatres and at court. He picked up ideas from books and from the world around him. Shakespeare's great skill is to have pleased an audience *and* written plays which tackle serious and universal themes. He did this while making them interesting, with various ideas and insights he picked up from all over his world.

FACTS

2 February 1603 *A Midsummer Night's Dream* performed at court.

17 May 1603 James I becomes Shakespeare's company's patron, the company is known as the King's Men.

1604 Shakespeare is living on Silver Street in London.

15 March 1604 Shakespeare and other King's Men players take part in James' coronation procession.

August 1604 Shakespeare and other King's Men players act as attendants to the Spanish Ambassador.

1 November 1604–12 February 1605 *Othello*, *Measure for Measure*, *Love's Labour's Lost*, *Henry V*, and *The Merchant of Venice* (twice) performed at court.

26 December 1606 *King Lear* performed at court.

1608 Shakespeare becomes a housekeeper (shareholder) in the Blackfriars Playhouse.

9 September 1608 Shakespeare's mother, Mary, is buried in Stratford.

Did Shakespeare retire?

We haven't found many questions about Shakespeare that have a simple answer, and the question of whether he retired is no different. We will look at his writing, and his life in London and Stratford, to get to our answer.

Writing plays

We have seen Shakespeare was slowing down. In the eight years from 1603 to 1610, he only produced 11 plays. This pattern continues. His 47th birthday was in April 1611, and he only wrote four plays in his remaining five years of life. What is more, three of these plays were collaborations with John Fletcher, who seems to have replaced him as the King's Men's resident playwright.

Some scholars suggest that *The Tempest*, the only one of the last four plays he wrote on his own, shows Shakepeare was thinking about retirement. The central character, Prospero, is a magician who has:

> be-dimmed
> *The noontide sun, called forth the mutinous winds,*

and

> *Graves at my command*
> *Have waked their sleepers, oped, and let 'em forth*
> *By my so potent art. But this rough magic*
> *I here abjure* [give up].[1]

It is very tempting to see this as Shakespeare describing his own life. As a great playwright he had made day feel like night; he *had* called forth storms and battles, and he *had* raised the dead, from Anthony and Cleopatra to Henry VII. "Rough magic" would be a great description for his work. But we should probably resist the temptation to read it as autobiography. Shakespeare went on after *The Tempest* to make the dead live again in *Henry VIII*, lovers fall madly in love in *Two Noble Kinsmen*, and we don't know what kind of magic in *Cardenio*, because the text is lost.

We can say the later plays tend to concentrate on the problems familiar to older people, but even so, in *The Two Noble Kinsmen*, the last play he wrote, he is again concerned with the erratic behaviour of young lovers.

Collaborators

John Fletcher was an up-and-coming playwright. He may have caught Shakespeare's attention by writing a sequel to *The Taming of the Shrew*, called *The Woman's Prize*.[2] In the original, set in Padua, Petruchio "tames" his violent and angry wife. In the sequel, after the death of his wife Petruchio moves to London, where his attempts to change the behaviour of his new wife, a Londoner, fail miserably. She tames *him*. We can't know whether this was a deliberate ploy to interest Shakespeare or not. If it was, it worked. In 1613–1614, they wrote three plays together.

Prospero (Roger Allam) just about to break his staff and give up magic, Shakespeare Globe 2013.

Shakespeare was also collaborating with Robert Johnson, a royal **lutenist** and composer. Johnson wrote songs for a number of Kings Men plays, including Shakespeare's *Cymbeline*, *The Winter's Tale*, *The Tempest*, and *Cardenio*. This fits with the greater importance of music in plays at the Blackfriars playhouse, as these are probably all of the plays Shakespeare wrote after the company started using it.

It wasn't a complete retirement from writing, at least until after 1614, but it might have been semi-retirement, with more time spent in Stratford.

Myth

The Tempest was Shakespeare's last play

This is an easy one to disprove. *The Tempest* was performed at the royal court on 1 November 1611. *Henry VIII* was first performed at the Globe in June 1613.

FACTS

Between 1611 and 1616, Shakespeare probably wrote:
The Tempest
Henry VIII (with John Fletcher)
Cardenio (with John Fletcher, lost)
The Two Noble Kinsmen (with John Fletcher)

Shakespeare's final London years

Plague hit London with unusual force in August 1608. The Council closed the theatres, and they did not reopen until late 1609 or early 1610. We don't know where Shakespeare spent this time, but it seems reasonable to infer he spent it out of London. During the closure, the King's Men did quite a bit of touring – we know they were in the Midlands, East Anglia, Oxford, and Kent. Shakespeare may have gone with the company on the tours, or he may have spent the time in Stratford. We can be reasonably certain he gave up acting before 1613, and perhaps before 1610.[3]

We know Shakespeare was in London for the Belott Mountjoy court case in May 1612, and he was there in March 1613, because he bought another property. This one was the gatehouse to the old Blackfriars monastery, very close to the Blackfriars Playhouse, and also close to the river where he could get a **wherry** to take him across to the Globe. There are a few odd things about this house purchase. The contract price was £140, but he would have paid more (see page 46). He didn't have all the money, and had to borrow £60. Also, he bought the house with three other men as trustees, given a joint responsibility to manage the property. It is tempting to see this as Shakespeare buying a perfectly placed London home, but he rented it out, so it seems to have been another investment.

There is no doubt about the next event. On 29 June 1613, during a performance of Shakespeare's new play, *Henry VIII*, the Globe burnt down. In a letter written to his nephew, Sir Henry Wotton described what happened:

> *certain chambers [cannon fired from an attic window in the tiring house] being shot off at his [Henry VIII's] entry, some of the paper ... wherewith one of them was stopped, did light on the thatch, where ... their eyes more attentive to the show, it kindled inwardly, and ran round ... consuming within less than an hour the whole house to the very grounds. This was the fatal period of that virtuous fabric, wherein yet nothing did perish, but wood and straw, and a very few forsaken cloaks; only one man had his breeches set on fire, that would perhaps have broiled him, if he had not by the benefit of a provident wit put it out with bottle ale.*[4]

The fire was such a talking point that ballads were printed describing it. They mention Burbage, Heminges, and Condell, but not Shakespeare. If he was there, he surely was famous enough to be mentioned, so we may infer he was not there, which suggests he had stopped acting by 1613.

The King's Men decided to rebuild the Globe, and each shareholder had to contribute £50–£60 to the rebuilding costs. We know Shakespeare was short of cash in March, when he needed a mortgage to buy the Blackfriars gatehouse. This may be why he took on the small job of designing a tournament shield and motto for the Earl of Rutland, for the small fee of 44 shillings, paid at the end of the month. Perhaps this is the moment he chose to sell his share in the Globe? As so often, there is no evidence.

Shakespeare certainly didn't stop visiting London. In November 1614, Thomas Greene wrote, "My cosen Shakespeare commying yesterday to towne I went to see him howe he did."[5] He was almost certainly in London in May 1615 for a court case about the Gatehouse property.

The most likely interpretation of this evidence is that Shakespeare hadn't cut all his connections to London, but he may well have spent less time there. He was still an investor and a man of the theatre, but probably a semi-retired one.

The rebuilt Globe Theatre had a tiled roof to prevent further fires. In 1647, the engraver mixed up the labels – the Globe is labelled *Beere Bayting* and the arena for Bear Baiting is labelled *The Globe*. The building to the left of the Globe is the tap house [bar] where the bottle of beer used on the burning breeches probably came from (see page 62).

Family matters

Shakespeare's elder daughter, Susanna, married on 5 June 1607. Her husband, John Hall, was a successful doctor. Their daughter, Elizabeth, baptized on 21 February 1608, was Shakespeare's first grandchild, the only one born while he was alive. William's two surviving brothers died in February 1612 and February 1613. This left William and his sister, Joan Hart, as the only surviving siblings.

Shakespeare had a bad summer in 1613. On 29 June, the Globe burnt down. On 15 July, the trouble was in Stratford. Susanna sued a local man, John Lane, for **slander**. Lane said she was unfaithful to Dr Hall and had a sexually transmitted disease. He offered no defence, and she won her case. Next year, on 9 July, a "suddaine and terrible Fire" destroyed 54 houses in Stratford as well as barns and stables – but all Shakespeare's property survived.[6]

The Welcome enclosure

In September 1614, three large landowners planned to enclose land around the small village of Welcome, where Shakespeare owned half the tithes. The villagers, supported by the Stratford Council, opposed the plan. Both sides wanted Shakespeare's support. He was an influential man in the town. In January 1615, work on boundary ditches started. Two councillors bought land in the fields, then because they were small landowners with rights, started to fill in the ditches. The enclosers' men stopped them and beat them. The next day, women and children from Stratford and the villages went out to fill the ditches. The enclosers couldn't face attacking them, so the scheme failed.

But what did Shakespeare do? On 28 October 1614, he made a private deal with the enclosers. If the value of his tithes fell because of the enclosures, they would compensate him. With his own finances secure, he did not support either side in public. At the height of the crisis, on 23 December, the Stratford Council wrote again, asking for his support. He seems to have done nothing.

What does this tell us about Shakespeare? He wasn't a community leader looking after the interests of the poor, and he wasn't a supporter of enclosure as a necessary change in farming. In his childhood, his father faced financial ruin, and the family must have been very short of money. As an adult, he seems to have been careful to build his family's wealth and status, and to hang on to it. This is important to remember when we look at his will.

Enclosures

"Open field" villages were made up of three huge fields divided into small strips, with some common land, which could be used by all for grazing. Some landowners had lots of land, some just a little, and landless labourers had none. This system could be inefficient. People could only have sheep, which was the most profitable thing to do, on the common land. Modernizers wanted to enclose – break the big fields and commons up into smaller fields. Each landowner got their share of fields. The farmers who got the fields could make more money. But it also caused poverty and hardship. Poor families, without much or any land, could no longer use the common land. Farmers raised more sheep and grew less grain. This hit the poor in two ways. Farmers needed hardly any workers to look after sheep, so there were fewer jobs, and there was less grain, so the price of bread went up.

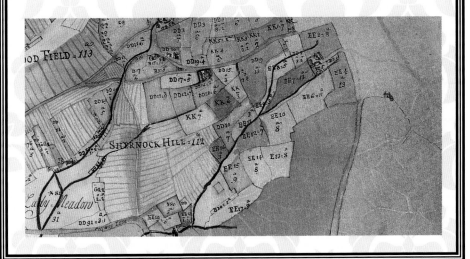

Judith's marriage

On 10 February 1616, Shakespeare's younger daughter, Judith, married Thomas Quiney. She was 31 – unusually old to marry. Thomas, four years younger than Judith, was not the perfect bridegroom. When he married Judith, another woman, Margaret Wheeler, was pregnant by him. She and her child both died in childbirth in March. Judith and her father may or may not have known before the wedding. They certainly knew in March, when Quiney was charged and found guilty of this crime in a church court. It may explain why Judith and Thomas were in a hurry to marry – they married in Lent when they needed a special licence, just as William and Anne had.

Shakespeare's will

At the time, people usually made their wills when they felt they were close to death. Shakespeare made a first draft of his will in January 1616. He changed it in March.[7] We don't know what the first draft said about Judith, but it is clear in March that Shakespeare didn't trust her husband Thomas. The main provisions for her in his will were:

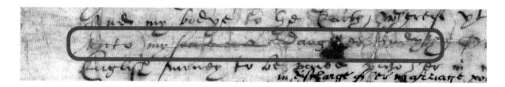

"unto my ~~Son in L~~ daughter Judyth"[8] – here we can see the lack of trust: *son-in-law* is crossed out, and the money left to Judith with very particular conditions: £100 to complete her dowry, £50 when she signed over her interest in the Chapel Lane cottage to Susanna, and £150, if she was alive in three years' time. This £150 was in the keeping of trustees, who would stop Thomas Quiney getting the money, only giving Judith the interest payments.

Joan Hart, his sister, got £20, all his "wearing Apparrell" (clothes to sell, or give to her sons) and to continue to live in the western part of the Birthplace, for nominal rent, 12 pence a year. Her three sons got £5 each.

Elizabeth Hall, his granddaughter, received "all my Plate", except a bowl that went to Judith. Plate meant his pewter and silver plates and dishes.

He gave "the Poore of Stratford" £10.

His Stratford friends were not forgotten – seven of them got small gifts.

He left "to my godson William Walker" £20/- in gold.

"my ffellowes John Hemynge Richard Burbage & Henry Cundell xxvjs viijd A peece to buy them Ringes" (the only people from his life in the theatre who are mentioned in his will).

All his property went to Susanna, **entailed** to her eldest son (if she had one), or if not, to her daughter Elizabeth, then to *her* eldest son. Clearly, Shakespeare wanted to create a single large estate that would always go to the eldest son. Susanna and her husband, John, also got "All the rest of my goodes chattels Leases plate Jewels & householde stuffe whatsoever". This included his books, and his theatre shares if he had not sold them earlier.

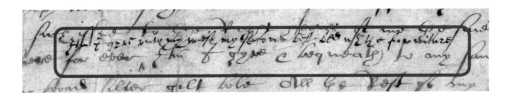

"Item I give unto my wife my second best bed with the furniture". As you can see, this was added between two lines. Does it mean that he had forgotten her? It could, but more likely it was added here because this bequest was originally on the first page, and when the first page was copied, it was missed out. This isn't the only thing he left her. She had her **dower right** under the law to live in New Place until she died, and to a third of the income he left to Susanna. And what about the "second best bed" part? It could have been their marriage bed. Interestingly, it could have been a bed from Anne's old home that needed to be returned.[9] As so often, we just don't know.

Myth   Shakespeare hated his wife

Many biographies assume Shakespeare was forced into marriage by Anne's pregnancy (perhaps purposely trapped by her cunning plan). The story goes on: they soon tired of one another, and he left Stratford after a couple of years of marriage. This interpretation is reinforced by the will in which all she gets is the second-best bed – and that seems an afterthought. This is possible, but it isn't the only story that fits the facts. There really aren't many facts about their married life. Anne was pregnant when they married, and she was in Stratford when their children were born. She died in Stratford in 1623. The only other thing we know is in his will in 1601, Thomas Whittington, who had been the Hathaway's shepherd, mentioned 40 shillings "that is in the hand of Anne Shaxpere". This is often interpreted as evidence that Shakespeare left Anne short of money, and she had to borrow. It is at least as likely that Whittington left the money in her care – she was the daughter of his old master, married to the successful Mr Shakespeare, and there were no banks at the time.

We don't know if Anne lived in Stratford or London. We don't know if the couple were miserable when they were apart, or when they were together. Perhaps William had plotted to marry Anne (she did have some money), and perhaps the creative, but careful, William depended on Anne's capable management of their lives. This fits the facts just as well.

Shakespeare's monuments

Shakespeare died on 23 April 1616. He was buried inside the church two days later. We don't know what caused his death. His sister Joan's husband had died the week before, and some historians think there was an outbreak of the disease we call typhus in the town that month.

We've seen in his will how Shakespeare wanted to consolidate his wealth in one estate, and pass it through the generations. His family decided to erect a monument suitable for the founder of a dynasty. It was made in Southwark, not far from the Globe, by Gheerart Janssen the younger. The family must have found it an acceptable likeness, because they used it in Stratford's church. This memorial bust (above) is one of only two authentic likenesses of Shakespeare. The monument hasn't had an easy history. Originally it was painted, but an 18th-century vicar whitewashed it, to make it look more dignified. On 2 October 1973, thieves cut the bust out from the wall looking for hidden manuscripts. They didn't find any, and the damage has been repaired.

FACTS

5 June 1607 Daughter Susanna marries John Hall, a doctor.
1611–12 *The Tempest* and *The Winter's Tale* performed at court.
May 1612 Shakespeare testifies at the Belott Mountjoy case in London.
1612–3 *Cardenio* (twice), *Henry IV Part 1*, *Much Ado*, *Winter's Tale*, *Julius Caesar*, *Tempest*, *Henry IV Part 2* performed at court.
10 March 1613 Shakespeare buys the Blackfriars gatehouse.
24 March 1613 Designs the Earl of Rutland's impressa, for 44 shillings.
29 June 1613 The Globe burns down during a performance of *Henry VIII*.
28 October 1614 Shakespeare does a private deal with the Welcome enclosers to protect his tithe income.
November and December 1614 Shakespeare in London for the Christmas court performances.
10 February 1616 Daughter Judith marries Thomas Quiney.
23 April 1616 Shakespeare dies in Stratford.

In fact, Shakespeare did not found a dynasty. Judith's children died young. Only Elizabeth, Susanna's daughter, lived to a good age. She married Thomas Nash, and then Sir John Bernard. She died, childless, in 1670.

The second authentic likeness of Shakespeare comes from his second monument: the book *Mr William Shakespeare's Comedies, Histories & Tragedies: Published according to the True Originall Copies*, which is usually called the *First Folio*. The 1623 edition is called *First* because it was reprinted three times in the next 62 years, each time with small changes, and *Folio* because that was the name of the size of this large book (made by folding a full standard sheet of paper in half).

The *First Folio* is vital to Shakespeare's reputation as a literary superstar. It contains 36 of his plays and is the only reason 18 survive. These include *The Tempest, Twelfth Night, Julius Caesar*, and *Macbeth*. John Heminges and Henry Condell, his fellow sharers and housekeepers, collected and arranged the publication of these "true originall copies". The King's Men owned the plays, and Heminges and Condell used the company's own manuscripts.

Shakespeare's reputation

Parliament shut all theatres in England in 1642, and they did not open again until 1660. In the 25 years between Shakespeare's death and the closure, he was not the literary superstar that he is now. His plays continued to be performed, but others were more popular. For example, we know the titles of many of the plays performed at court. During these 25 years, 16 were Shakespeare's, but 50 were by Fletcher (often with a collaborator). However, as others' reputations diminished, Shakespeare's grew.

Epilogue

How do we sum up Shakespeare? I think some consistent themes come through the story we have been looking at.

He was steeped in the theatre – as an actor, a playwright, a company sharer, and part owner of two theatres. You can't make a convincing historical case for Shakespeare not writing the plays. There's too much evidence that he did – his connections with the theatre and plays at court, how his wealth grew, the repeated references to him as a playwright, all fit together. Historians evaluate their evidence, and then follow it. The only way anybody can argue Shakespeare didn't write the plays is by saying it was a conspiracy, that everybody else at the time was fooled, and Shakespeare was paid to pretend to be the author. This isn't history. It is the worst kind of unsupported inference or invention. It is like a conspiracy theory, with the same lack of factual basis as stories about alien abductions or the existence of unicorns.

This is from the play-within-the-play in *A Midsummer Night's Dream*. Bottom (playing Pyramus) tries to kiss Flute (playing Thisbe) through a hole in the wall (played by Snout). It is one of those moments that suggest the author knew exactly what worked on stage.

Shakespeare was careful with money, and determined to die a rich man, leaving a significant estate to his (hopefully male) descendants. He wasn't a perfect person. The idea of a "role model" is a modern one – another anachronism. It would be nice to think of Shakespeare as caring and daring, but in his financial dealings, he can seem selfish. If he did change his story in the Belott Mountjoy case, he abandoned Belott and his wife Mary. He did less than most other prominent citizens of Stratford to help the poor in the Welcome enclosure case.

We have lots of evidence about Shakespeare, but most of the time it doesn't tell us what we want to know. When we don't know, we must accept this, not speculate or invent. Shakespeare's books are a good example. Scholars have tracked dozens of books he must have read, because he quotes from them, or they clearly influence what he wrote. Yet there are no books mentioned in his will. But then the inventory of his goods that went with the will is lost, and everything went to Susanna and John Hall, so there was no need to mention individual items. So the correct conclusion is not that he had no books, but that we don't know what books he had.

Myth   The Earl of Oxford wrote Shakespeare's plays

Why don't I, the author, believe the Earl of Oxford wrote the plays?

- The idea that Shakespeare wasn't educated enough because he didn't go to university is an anachronism. We saw, when we looked at his schooling, that the Elizabethan grammar school gave an extensive classical education. Students had to read, write, and learn by heart Latin text.
- The idea that he didn't travel enough, or mix in high enough society to write the plays is also a mistake. It is part of the mistake of thinking the plays are autobiographical. They are works of the imagination. Shakespeare could mix with all sorts of people in London, and he had access to a wide range of books.
- Oxford died on 24 June 1604. Fifteen of the plays were written after this, and as we have seen, many fit in with the changes in politics and the new indoor theatre.
- The plays show a consistent understanding of what works on stage, and a development of skill and technique. This fits the facts of the life of the actor and theatrical shareholder William Shakespeare, not the aristocratic Earl of Oxford.

Timeline

1564	Born *c.* 23 April, Stratford, Warwickshire
1576	*The Theatre, London's first permanent playhouse, opens*
1582	*c.* 28 November, marries Anne Hathaway
1583	26 May, daughter Susanna Shakespeare baptized
1584	*First English colonists land at Roanoke in Virginia, America*
1585	2 February, twins Hamnet and Judith Shakespeare baptized
1592	3 March, *Henry VI Part 1* first performed at the Rose Theatre
	20 September, criticized in Greene's *Groats-worth of Witte*
1593	February, poem *Venus and Adonis* published
1594	May, poem *The Rape of Lucrece* published
	Becomes a sharer in the Lord Chamberlain's Men
1596	Christmas, *Henry IV Part 1* performed at court
1597	15 November, listed as not having paid his taxes (5 shillings)
1598	4 February, listed as having 80 bushels of malt in Stratford
	7 September, Francis Meres praises Shakespeare's poems and plays
	1 October, listed as having not paid a tax bill (13 shillings 4 pence)
1599	Moves to Bankside in London
	Summer, the Globe Theatre opens with Shakespeare as a shareholder
1603	2 February, *Midsummer Night's Dream* performed at court
	March, Elizabeth I dies, James I becomes King of England
	17 May, Shakespeare's company becomes the King's Men
1604	Shakespeare is living in Silver Street in London
	15 March, Shakespeare and King's Men in the coronation procession
	In Stratford, sells Philip Rogers 20 bushels of malt worth £2 on credit
1605	24 July, buys a half interest in tithes outside Stratford for £440
	5 November Gunpowder Plot fails
1607	5 June, daughter Susanna marries John Hall, a doctor
1608	17 August, sues Richard Addenbroke of Stratford for debt
1611–12	*The Tempest* and *The Winter's Tale* performed at court
1612	May, testifies at the Belott Mountjoy case in London
1612–13	*Cardenio, Henry IV Part 1, Much Ado, The Winter's Tale, Julius Caesar, Tempest, Henry IV Part 2* performed at court
1613	10 March, buys the Blackfriars Gatehouse
	24 March, designs the Earl of Rutland's "impressa", for 44 shillings
	29 June, the Globe burns down during a performance of *Henry VIII*
1614	28 October, makes deal with the Welcome enclosers to protect tithe income
	November and December, in London
1616	10 February, daughter Judith marries Thomas Quiney in Stratford
	23 April, dies in Stratford
1623	*First Folio* published

Money then and now

The table below picks out some prices and wages from around 1600, during Shakespeare's lifetime, and compares them with current prices and wages. The central section shows you the 1600 price multiplied by the figure at the top of the column. So 1d (one penny) multiplied by 200 would be 83 pence, multiplied by 300 £1.25, and so on. The figures in bold show you the best comparison between prices then and now. As you can see, no single multiplier gives an accurate conversion to current prices, even for this small range of things. Most people, including children, drank beer as their normal drink. Tea and coffee were unknown, and water was not always safe to drink.

| | c. 1600 | Multiply by | | | | | | | 2013 price |
		200	300	500	800	2000	3000	5000	
pint of beer	½ d	£0.42	£0.63	£1.04	£1.67	**£4.17**	£6.25	£10.42	£3.50
loaf of bread	1d	**£0.83**	**£1.25**	£2.08	£3.33	£8.33	£12.50	£20.83	85p–£1.35
cheapest entry, Globe	1d	£0.83	£1.25	£2.08	£3.33	£8.33	**£12.50**	£20.83	£12.00
cheapest entry, Blackfriars	6d	£5.00	£7.50	£12.50	**£20.00**	£50.00	£75.00	£125.00	£25.00
book of a new play	6d	£5.00	**£7.50**	£12.50	£20.00	£50.00	£75.00	£125.00	£9.99
rent a horse/car for a day	12d	£10.00	£15.00	**£25.00**	**£40.00**	£100.00	£150.00	£250.00	£33.66
copy of the First Folio	£1	**£200.00**	£300.00	£500.00	£800.00	£2,000.00	£3,000.00	£5,000.00	£150.00
Salaries									
Baker	£4 13s 6d	£935	£1,403	£2,338	£3,740	£9,350	£14,025	**£23,375**	£24,000
Stratford school master /modern headteacher	£20	£4,000	£6,000	£10,000	£16,000	£40,000	£60,000	**£100,000**	£85–100,000

Glossary

abdicate when a monarch gives up their throne

apprentice youth who has a contract to learn a trade

armoury place where weapons and armour are stored

auditorium part of a theatre where the audience are

banns announcement that a marriage is planned, giving time to object for any person who knows a reason why it should not be allowed

birch bundle of sticks used for beating people

bond money that is paid as security for something

capital large sums of money saved or invested

court household of the monarch, including government ministers, and everyone who lived and worked there

discovery space central opening in the tiring house wall at the back of the stage which could be opened to reveal things to the audience

doublet jacket with removable sleeves

dower right right of a widow to live in the family home and have one third of her dead husband's income

dowry property or money the bride's family gives to the husband

empathy ability to see another person's point of view

entail legal procedure to leave an inheritance to particular heirs (for example, the eldest son in each generation) and to stop it being broken up

epilogue section at the end of a play or book that acts as a conclusion

executor person responsible for seeing a will is carried out as the dead person intended

favourite courtier given many gifts by the king, often more than their service is worth

gable triangular upper part of a wall at the end of a roof

gallery (usually three) tiers of seats in a playhouse

guild company of people from the same trade who regulate the way the trade can be carried out

heresy religious belief which is against the beliefs of the state church

hierarchical organized by class from the top (king) to the lowest (homeless beggar)

holy day saint's day. In Shakespeare's time, these were public holidays.

housekeeper in Shakespeare's theatre, a shareholder in a theatre building

infer to come to a conclusion by using reasoning rather than facts

Jacobean from the reign of James I

lath and plaster strips of wood, plastered on the outside, used to make walls and ceilings in buildings

lease legal document renting property for a given number of years

lutenist person who plays the lute, a stringed instrument

Muses in Greek myths, the nine goddesses of the Arts

original practices style of production pioneered at Shakespeare's Globe by Mark Rylance and his team to recreate the costume and music Shakespeare's audiences would have recognized

parish small district with its own church and clergy; sometimes a unit of local government based on it

patron person who gives support or protection, often financial

pirate edition book printed and sold by people who did not have the right to do so

polygonal many-sided

Puritan strict Protestant in religion, somebody who wanted a more godly society, with rules enforcing good behaviour

Reformation change in official Church from Roman Catholic to Protestant. At the time, all people in the country were forced to worship only in the official Church.

rhetoric using words persuasively; also can be used to describe exaggerated language

royal patent permission given by a monarch to an acting company, allowing them to perform

sharer in English theatre 1576–1642, a shareholder in a company of players

shroud cloth a dead person is wrapped in for burial

Shrove short for Shrovetide, the three days in the Christian calendar before the start of Lent. It was used for merrymaking and excess in Shakespeare's time.

sibling brother and/or sister

slander in law, to speak lies about another person

sonnet 14-line poem with a set rhyme scheme

soliloquy speech by an actor directly to the audience, usually about feelings or plans

speculator one who makes risky investments hoping for large profits

stage trap trapdoor in the stage which could be opened to let devils enter, be a grave, and so on

sturdy beggar legal description of a person who was fit to work, but was begging, not working

synonym word with the same or similar meaning as another word

tenant person renting a property

tiring house in England 1576–1642, the part of the theatre behind the stage, where the actors dressed and waited to go on stage, and where the companies' play books and costumes were stored

treason in law, the crime of betraying your country or monarch

usurer person who lends money for (usually high) interest

wherry light rowing boat that acted as a water taxi on the River Thames

whittawer somebody who tanned leather and dealt in luxury goods

Source references

Who was Shakespeare? (4–5)

1. www.telegraph.co.uk/comment/columnists/
borisjohnson/8600125/Shakespeare-torchbearer-
for-the-Chinese-way-of-doing-things.html
[accessed 9 February 2013].
2. Elise Broach, *Shakespeare's Secret* (London:
Walker Books, 2006) 42. I owe this reference to
the best modern account of the controversy about
who wrote the plays, James Shapiro's *Contested
Will: Who wrote Shakespeare?* (London: Faber and
Faber, 2010).

Where did Shakespeare come from? (6–12)

1. S. Schoenbaum, *William Shakespeare: A
Documentary Life* (Oxford: OUP, 1975), 13–15.
The fine is in the records of the Stratford Town
Council.
2. *Ibid*, 18; shaksper.net/archive/2005/225-
march/22532-john-jordans-book.
3. *Ibid*, 24; and Bill Bryson, *Shakespeare: The
World as a Stage* (London: Harper Perennial,
2008), 23–4.
4. You can see the page at findingshakespeare.
co.uk/going-digital-the-birth-and-burial-records-
of-william-shakespeare/sbt_bs_ws36_dr243_1_p2.
5. Bill Bryson, *Shakespeare: The World as a Stage*,
37–8.
6. *Ibid*, 38

After school... marriage (12–17)

1. S. Schoenbaum, *William Shakespeare: A
Documentary Life*, 36–8; and Stephen Greenblatt,
Will in the World (London: Jonathan Cape, 2004),
57–60.
2. S. Schoenbaum, *William Shakespeare: A
Documentary Life*, 41.
3. *Ibid*, 46
4. *Ibid*, 62
5. *Ibid*, 70. The original is in Latin.
6. *Ibid*, 63. The original is in Latin.
7. Bill Bryson, *Shakespeare: The World as a Stage*,
40.
8. Stephen Greenblatt, *Will in the World*, 118–19;
and S. Schoenbaum, *William Shakespeare: A
Documentary Life*, 75–6.

What happened next? (18–21)

1. The earliest versions of this story are tracked
down in S. Schoenbaum, *William Shakespeare: A
Compact Documentary Life*, 97–99. Michael Wood,
In Search of Shakespeare (London: BBC Books,
2005), 106–8, looks at how the story might
contain a grain of truth.
2. Quoted in Michael Wood, *In Search of
Shakespeare*, 59.

Moving to London (22–33)

1. This is based on a translation by Clare
Williams. To read Platter's full account of his time
in England see Peter Razzell, ed., *The Journals
of Two Travellers in Elizabethan and Early Stuart
England* (London: Caliban Books, 1995).
2. Julian Bowsher, *Shakespeare's London
Theatreland* (London: Museum of London
Archaeology, 2012), 68–80.
3. S. Schoenbaum, *William Shakespeare: A
Documentary Life*, 116.
4. In *Kind Heart's Dream*, 1592, quoted
in S. Schoenbaum, *William Shakespeare: A
Documentary Life*, 117.
5. R.A. Foakes, *Henslowe's Diary, 2nd ed.*
(Cambridge: CUP, 2002), 16–9.
6. Michael Wood, *In Search of Shakespeare*, 149,
estimates 1,634 in the galleries, and says that
should be more than doubled to allow for the
yard. So my calculation is: over 30,000 saw the
play, and the population of London was 200,000
(see note 1 on page 22).
7. E.K. Chambers, *The Elizabethan Stage*, 4 vols
(Oxford: Clarendon Press, 1945), IV, 199.
8. S. Schoenbaum, *William Shakespeare: A
Compact Documentary Life*, 126.
9. For the different theatres in London, and
where they were, see Jane Shuter, *Shakespeare
and the Theatre* (Oxford: Raintree, 2014), 11; and
Wendy Greenhill, *Shakespeare's Theatre, 2nd ed.*
(Oxford: Heinemann, 2007), 5–19.

What makes Shakespeare different? (34–43)

1. S. Schoenbaum, *William Shakespeare: A
Documentary Life*, 140.
2. Robert Parker Sorlien, ed., *The Diary of John
Manningham of the Middle Temple, 1602–1603*,
(Boston: University Press of New England, 1976),
75.
3. For a fuller description of problems posed by
the sonnets, see Bryson, *Shakespeare: The World as
a Stage*, 137–46 and Michael Wood, *In Search of*

Shakespeare, 188–200.

4. S. Schoenbaum, *William Shakespeare: A Documentary Life*, 140–1.

5. special-1.bl.uk/treasures/SiqDiscovery/ui/record.aspx?Source=text&LHCopy=96&LHPage=80&RHCopy=96&RHPage=81.

6. *King John*, Act 3, Scene 3, lines 95–6.

7. To find out more about this read Laurie Maguire and Emma Smith, *30 Great Myths About Shakespeare* (Oxford: Wiley-Blackwell, 2013), 113–18.

8. For a map of London's theatres see Jane Shuter, *Shakespeare and the Theatre* (Raintree, 2014), p. 11.

9. S. Schoenbaum, *William Shakespeare: A Documentary Life*, 153.

10. This is based on a translation by Clare Williams. To read Platter's full account of his time in England see Peter Razzell, ed., *The Journals of Two Travellers in Elizabethan and Early Stuart England*, (London: Caliban Books, 1995).

11. S. Schoenbaum, *William Shakespeare: A Documentary Life*, 160.

Was Shakespeare rich? (44–49)

1. S. Schoenbaum, *William Shakespeare: A Documentary Life*, 153.

2. *Ibid*, 166–171.

3. *Ibid*, 171–3.

4. I am grateful to Philip Hall, agricultural valuer at Savills Banbury office, for the modern valuation.

5. S. Schoenbaum, *William Shakespeare: A Documentary Life*, 161–3.

6. *Ibid*, 179, 184

7. *Ibid*, 192

The King's man (50–59)

1. E.K. Chambers, *The Elizabethan Stage*, II, 208.

2. S. Schoenbaum, *William Shakespeare: A Documentary Life*, 196.

3. Words in quotes are Shakespeare's, either from his testimony, or the testimony of Daniel Nicholas about his conversation with Shakespeare. From Charles Nicholl, *The Lodger: Shakespeare on Silver Street* (London: Allen Lane, 2007), 288–90.

4. I owe the idea, and the example, to Stephen Greenblatt, *Will in the World*, 323–9.

Did Shakespeare retire? (60–69)

1. *The Tempest*, Act 5, Scene 1, lines 46–7, 53–56.

2. The play was originally published with a subtitle, *The Woman's Prize or the Tamer Tamed*. It has been rescued from neglect in the 21st century, with a production at the RSC in 2003, and two modern editions of the play. All three reversed the title, calling the play *The Tamer Tamed*, because its connection to *The Taming of the Shrew* is good marketing.

3. S. Schoenbaum, William Shakespeare: *A Documentary Life*, 147–52; Andrew Gurr, *The Shakespeare Company* (Cambridge University Press, 2004), 60.

4. E.K. Chambers, *The Elizabethan Stage*, II, 419–20.

5. Charles Nicholl, *The Lodger: Shakespeare on Silver Street*, 38.

6. From a letter written on behalf of the Stratford Town Council, S. Schoenbaum, *William Shakespeare: A Documentary Life*, 230.

7. Studies of Shakespeare's will suggest he made a second draft in March, when the whole first page was written again, and by a copying mistake January was left as the date. Pages two and three just had some crossings out, and additions written between the existing lines. S. Schoenbaum, *William Shakespeare: A Documentary Life*, 242–6.

8. All words in quotation marks are direct quotes from his will, S. Schoenbaum, *William Shakespeare: A Documentary Life*, 242–5.

9. In his will, Anne's father, Richard Hathaway, mentions two beds: "Item ... the two joined-beds in my parlour, shall continue and stand unmoved during the natural life ... of Joan my wife, and the natural life of Bartholomew my son, and John my son, and the longest liver of them". So these beds were Hathaway heirlooms. Perhaps Anne had taken one to Stratford? There was only one in the Hathaway house in an inventory taken when Bartholomew died in 1624, but two again when the descendants of Richard finally left the house in the 19th century. If Anne had taken one of these beds, it would need to be clear in the will it should not go to Susanna with all the other furniture. So this clause might have been included because Anne remembered and wanted it in. This is a nice story, and obviously speculation – but no more speculation than the interpretation that sees the second-best bed as intentional rudeness from William to Anne. Michael Wood, *In Search of Shakespeare*, 374–5.

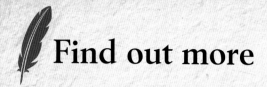

Find out more

Books

In Search of Shakespeare, Michael Wood, this is both a book (BBC Books, 2005) and a TV series available on DVD (BBC, 2003)

Shakespeare and the Theatre, Jane Shuter (Raintree, 2014)

Shakespeare's London Theatreland: Archaeology, History and Drama, Julian Bowsher (Museum of London, 2012)

Shakespeare, Man of the Theatre, Wendy Greenhill and Paul Wignall (Heinemann Library, 1999)

Shakespeare: The World as a Stage, Bill Bryson (Harper Collins, 2007)

The Lodger: Shakespeare on Silver Street, Charles Nicholl (Penguin, 2009)

William Shakespeare: A Compact Documentary Life, S. Schoenbaum (OUP, 1987)

Websites

www.shakespeare.org.uk

The Shakespeare Birthplace Trust runs the Shakespeare properties, which you can visit if you can get to Stratford.

www.folger.edu

The Folger Shakespeare Library has a First Folio and other important documents available to look at online.

The plays

The best thing is to go and see Shakespeare's plays performed live – this is what Shakespeare was writing for.

- *Globe Education Shakespeare* (Hodder Education, 2011 onwards) has lots of photos, gives a sense of the plays in performance, and has very good notes.
- *The Folger* Shakespeare series (Washington Square Press) has good notes.
- Shakespeare's Globe in London produces plays in the summer in the Globe, and in the winter in its indoor theatre. It is now issuing DVDs of many productions. See their website: www.shakespearesglobe.com
- The Royal Shakespeare Company produces plays in two Stratford theatres all year. It occasionally issues DVDs of a production: www.rsc.org.uk

Index